PIANO • VOCAL • GUITAR

CHRISTMAS POP STANDARDS

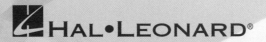

ISBN 978-1-70510-292-3

Visit Hal Leonard Online at
www.halleonard.com

Contact Us:
Hal Leonard
7777 West Bluemound Road
Milwaukee, WI 53213
Email: info@halleonard.com

In Europe, contact:
Hal Leonard Europe Limited
42 Wigmore Street
Marylebone, London, W1U 2RN
Email: info@halleonardeurope.com

In Australia, contact:
Hal Leonard Australia Pty. Ltd.
4 Lentara Court
Cheltenham, Victoria, 3192 Australia
Email: info@halleonard.com.au

ALL I WANT FOR CHRISTMAS IS YOU

Words and Music by MARIAH CAREY
and WALTER AFANASIEFF

- re - place. _____ / Santa Claus won't make ___ me hap - py
___ Saint Nick. _____ / I won't e - ven stay ___ a - wake __ to
- ing for. _____ / I just want to see ___ my ba - by

with a toy _____ on Christ - mas day. ____
hear those ___ mag - ic rein - deer click. ___
stand - ing right ___ out - side _____ my door. ___

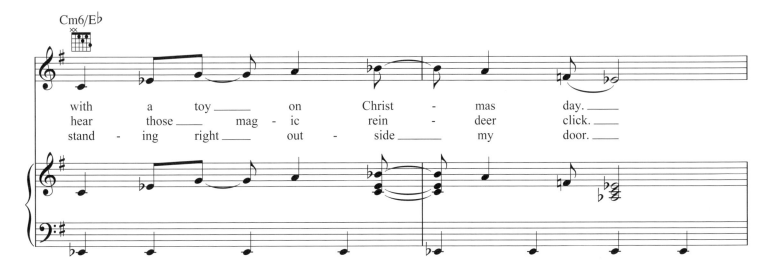

I just want you for ___ my own, __ more than you could ev -
I just want you here ___ to - night, __ hold - ing on to me ___
I just want him for ___ my own, __ more than you could ev -

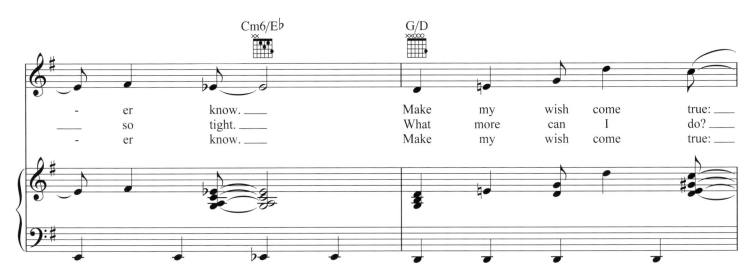

- er know. ___ / Make my wish come true: ___
___ so tight. ___ / What more can I do? ___
- er know. ___ / Make my wish come true: ___

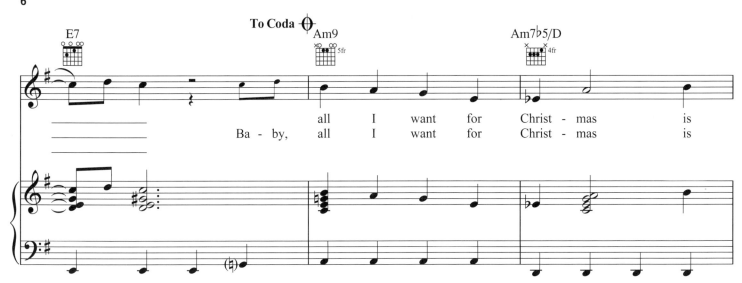

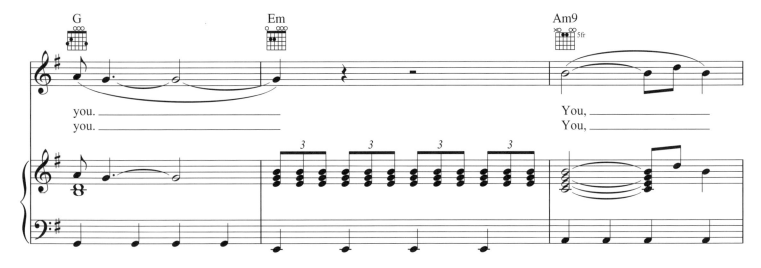

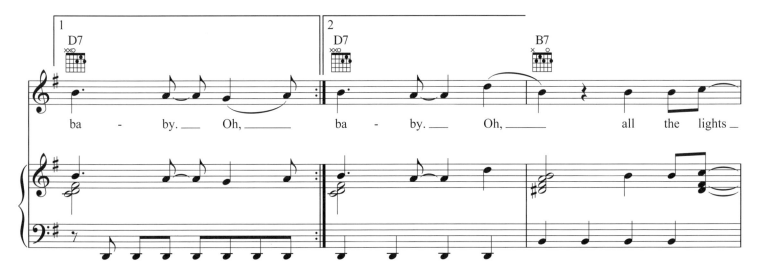

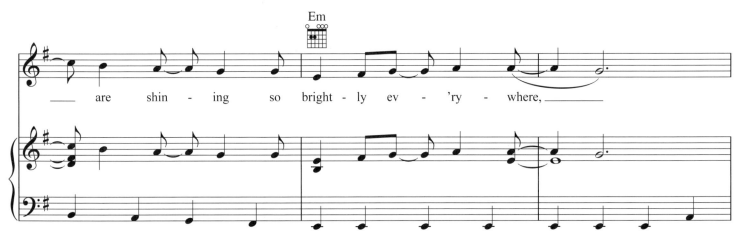

and the sound ___ of chil - dren's laugh - ter fills ___ the air, ___

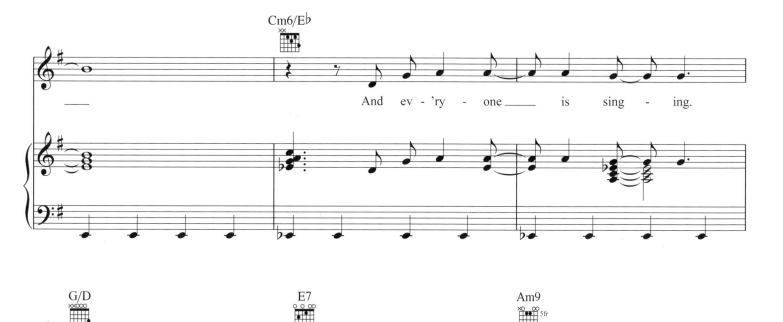

___ And ev - 'ry - one ___ is sing - ing.

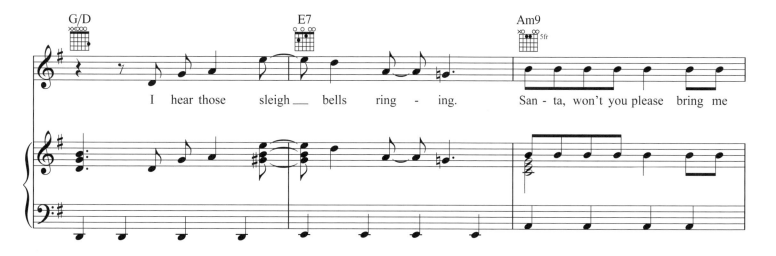

I hear those sleigh ___ bells ring - ing. San - ta, won't you please bring me

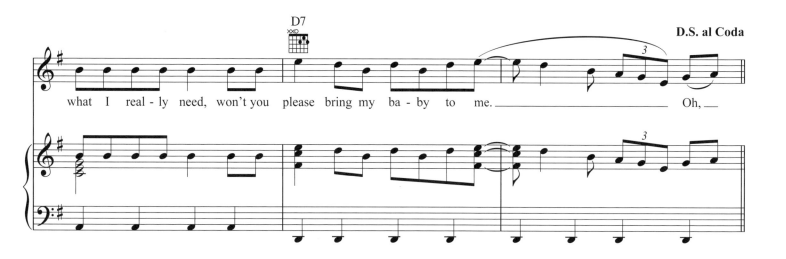

what I real - ly need, won't you please bring my ba - by to me. ___ Oh, ___

D.S. al Coda

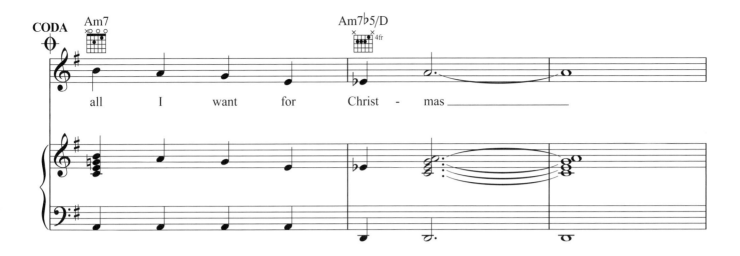

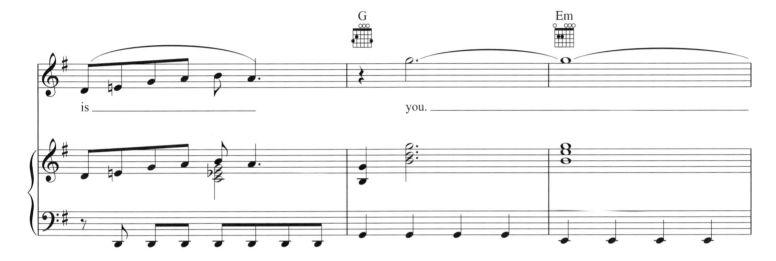

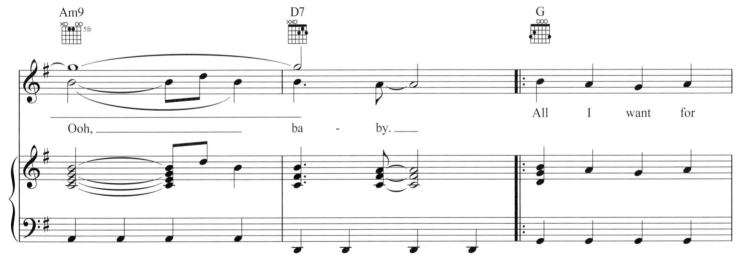

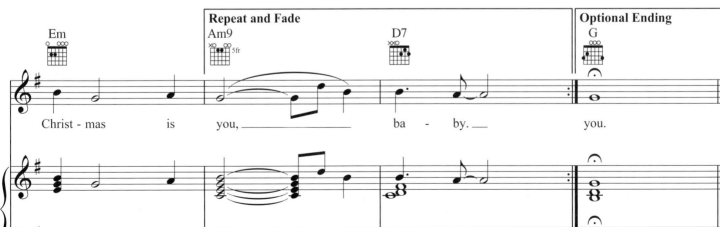

BELIEVE

from Warner Bros. Pictures' THE POLAR EXPRESS

Words and Music by GLEN BALLARD
and ALAN SILVESTRI

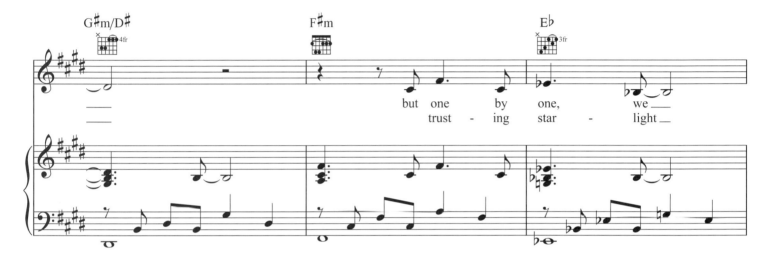

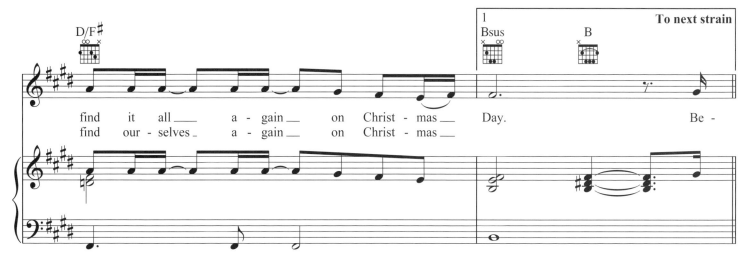

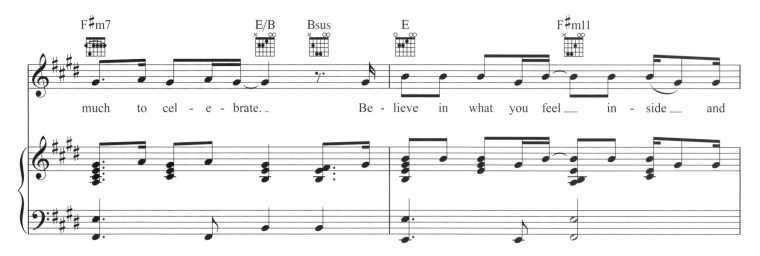

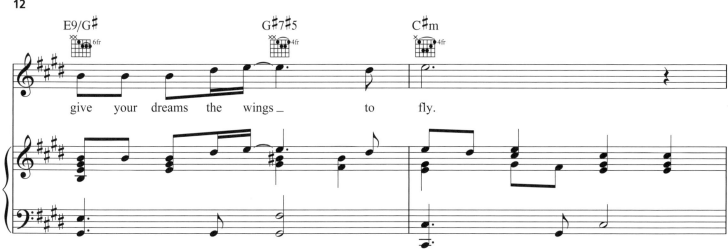

give your dreams the wings _____ to fly.

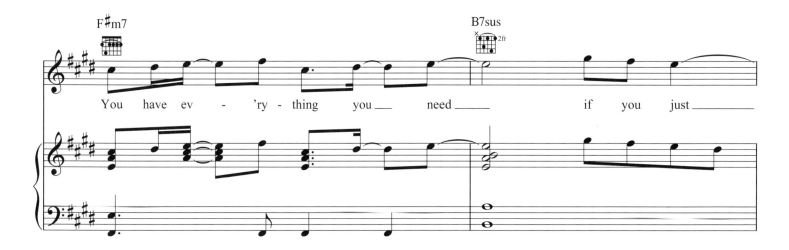

You have ev - 'ry - thing you _____ need _____ if you just _____

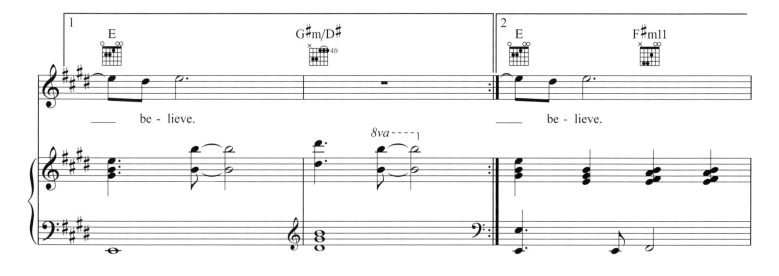

_____ be - lieve.   _____ be - lieve.

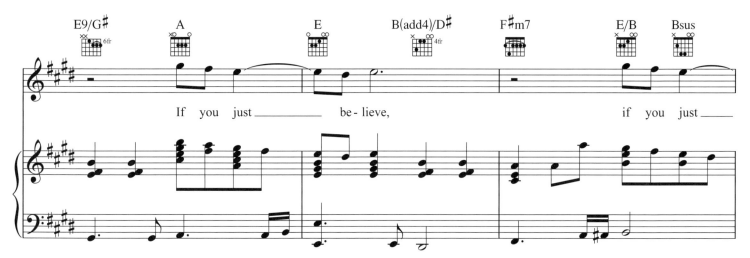

If you just _____ be - lieve,   if you just _____

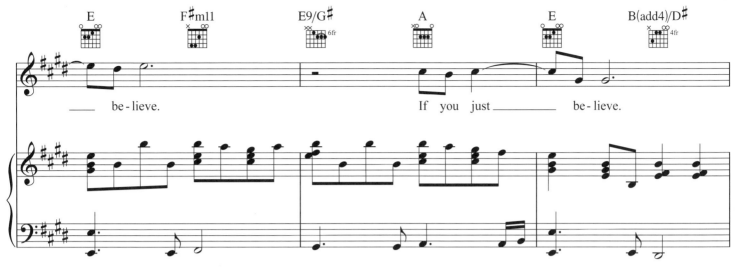

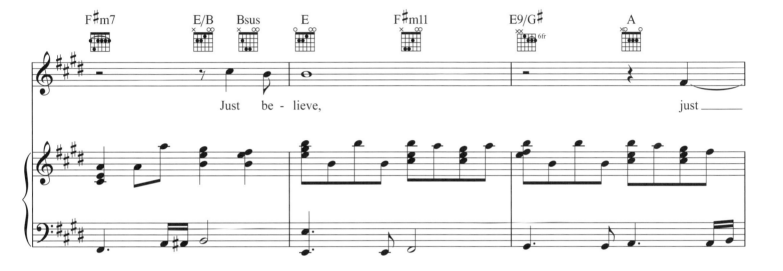

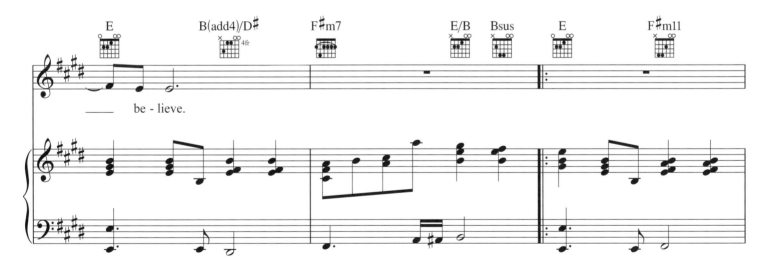

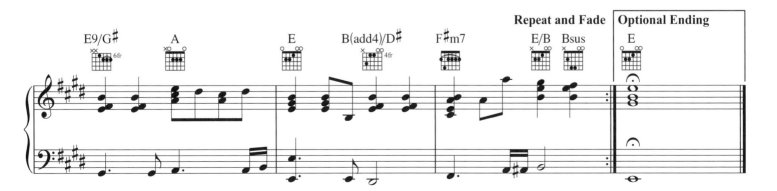

BLUE CHRISTMAS

Words and Music by BILLY HAYES
and JAY JOHNSON

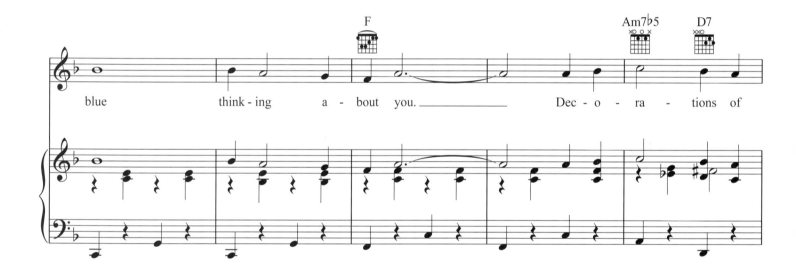

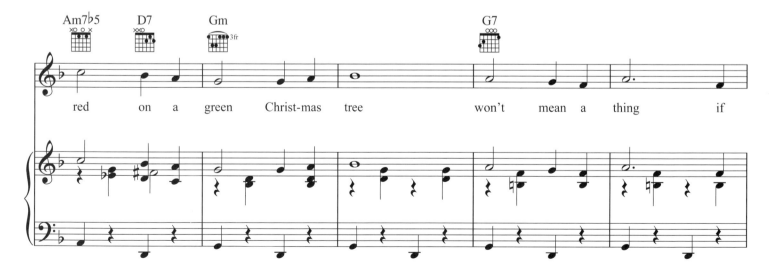

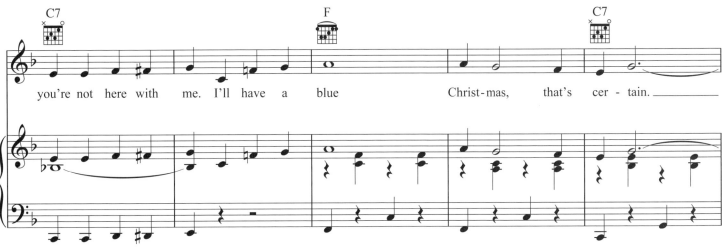

you're not here with me. I'll have a blue Christ-mas, that's cer - tain.____

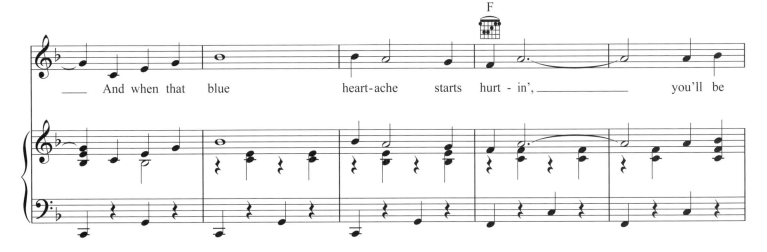

____ And when that blue heart-ache starts hurt - in',_____ you'll be

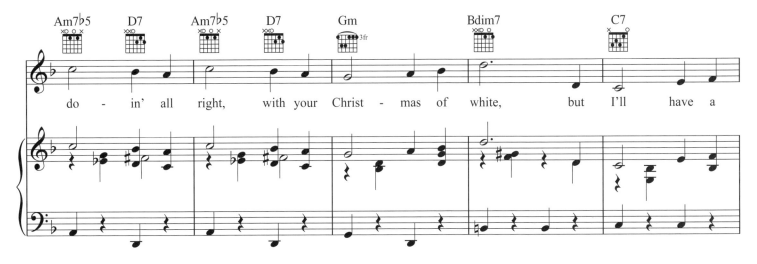

do - in' all right, with your Christ - mas of white, but I'll have a

blue, blue Christ - mas._____ I'll have a Christ - mas.____

CHRISTMAS
(Baby Please Come Home)

Words and Music by PHIL SPECTOR,
ELLIE GREENWICH and JEFF BARRY

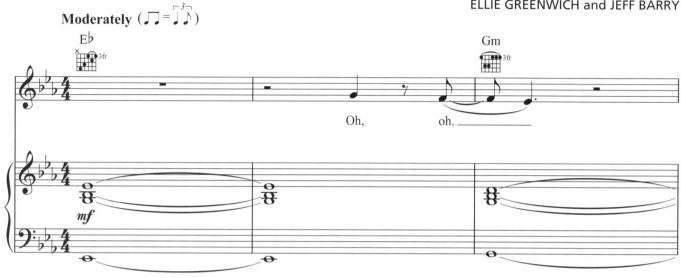

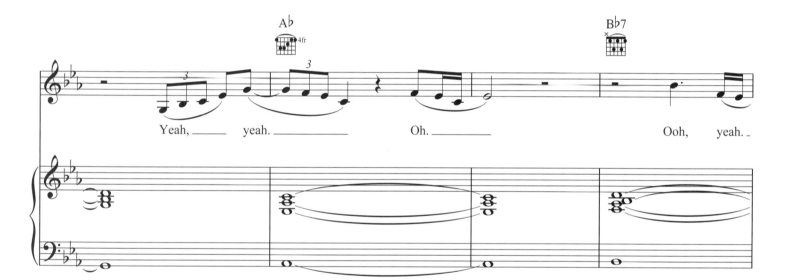

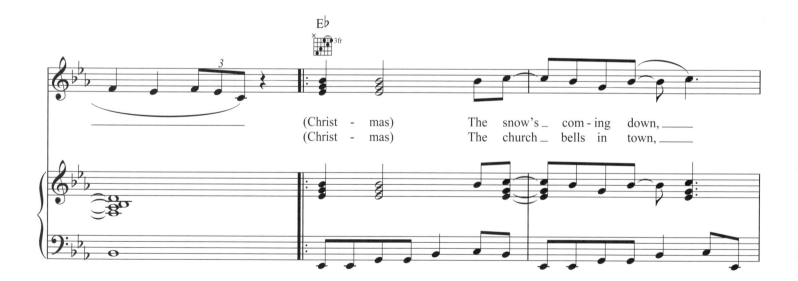

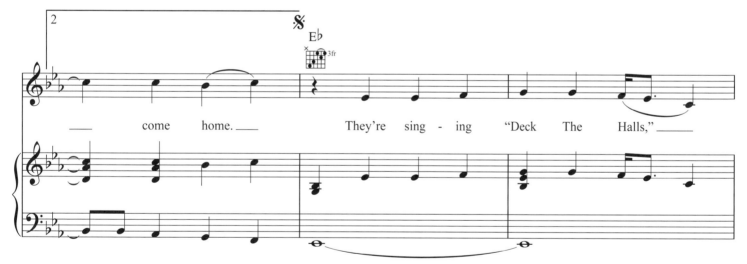

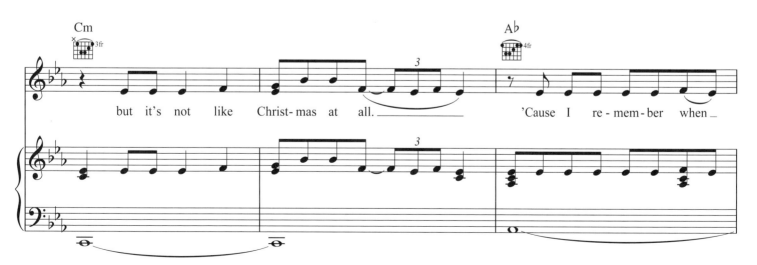

you were here ___ and all the fun we had ___ last year. ___

(Christ - mas) Pret - ty lights ___ on the tree, ___ (Christ - mas) I'm

Instrumental solo

(Christ - mas) If there ___ was a way ___ (Christ - mas) I'd

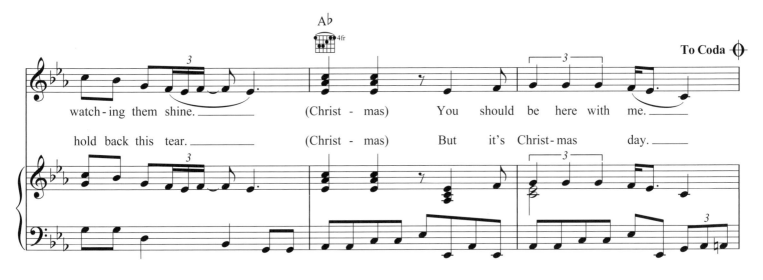

To Coda

watch - ing them shine. ___ (Christ - mas) You should be here with me.

hold back this tear. ___ (Christ - mas) But it's Christ - mas day. ___

D.S. al Coda

(Christ - mas) Ba - by please ___ come home. ___ *Solo ends*

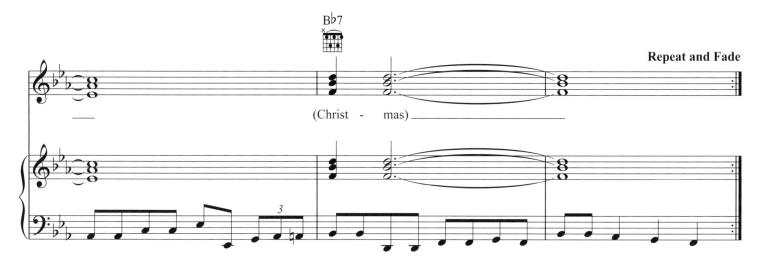

DO YOU HEAR WHAT I HEAR

Words and Music by NOEL REGNEY
and GLORIA SHAYNE

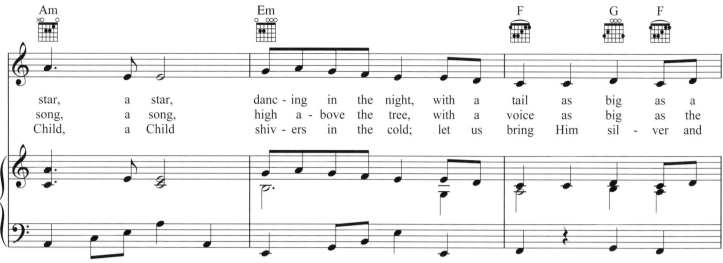

star, a star, danc - ing in the night, with a tail as big as a
song, a song, high a - bove the tree, with a voice as big as the
Child, a Child shiv - ers in the cold; let us bring Him sil - ver and

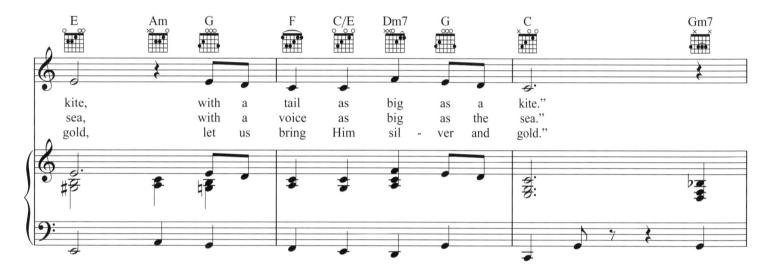

kite, with a tail as big as a kite."
sea, with a voice as big as the sea."
gold, let us bring Him sil - ver and gold."

Said the
Said the Said the king to the peo - ple ev - 'ry -

where, "Lis - ten to what I say! _____

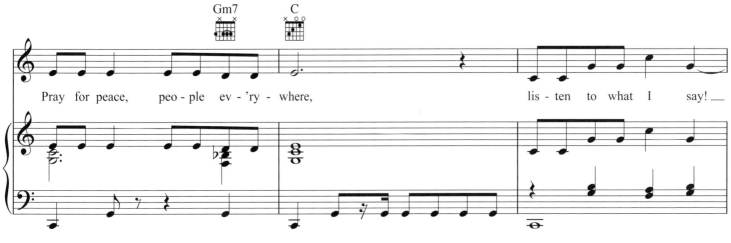

Pray for peace, peo - ple ev - 'ry - where, lis - ten to what I say! __

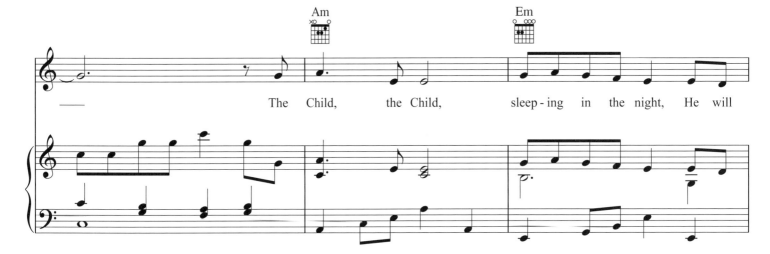

__ The Child, the Child, sleep - ing in the night, He will

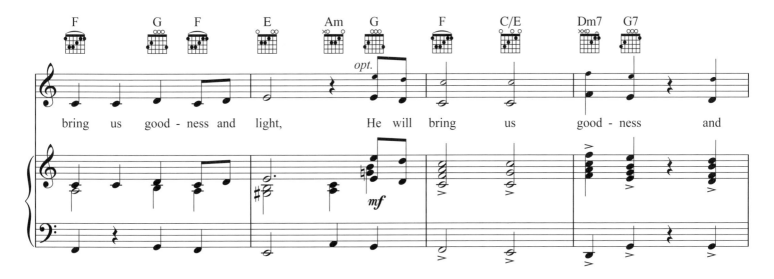

bring us good - ness and light, He will bring us good - ness and

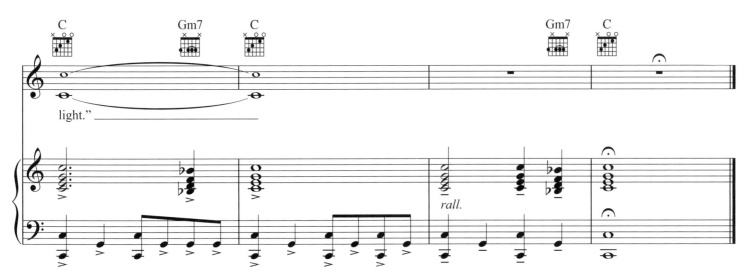

light." _____

CHRISTMAS TIME IS HERE

from A CHARLIE BROWN CHRISTMAS

Words by LEE MENDELSON
Music by VINCE GUARALDI

Christ - mas time is here, hap - pi - ness and
Snow - flakes in the air, car - ols ev - 'ry -

cheer. Fun for all that chil - dren call their
where. Old - en times and an - cient rhymes of

fa - v'rite time of year.
love and dreams to share.

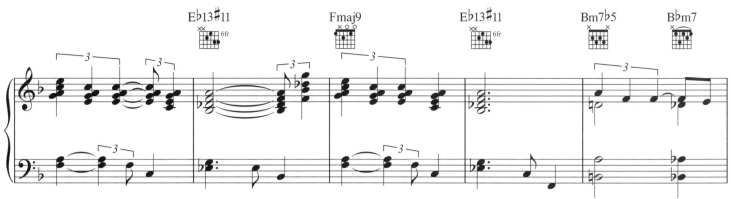

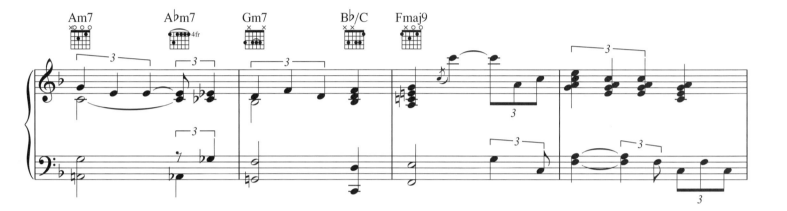

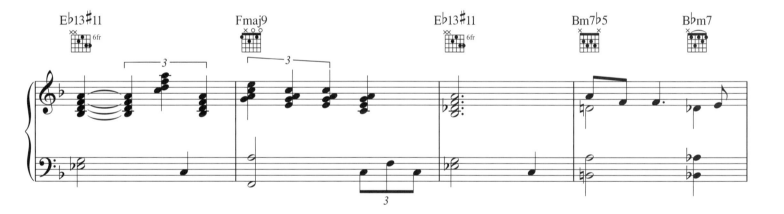

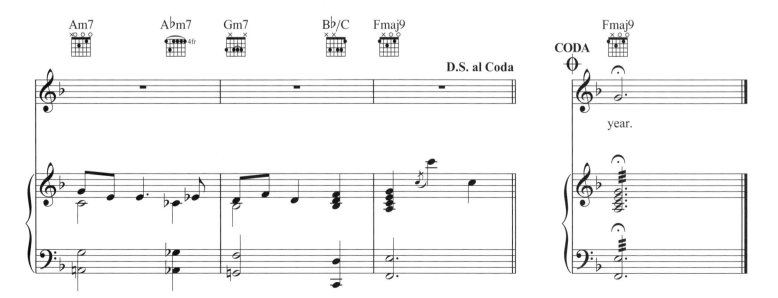

GROWN-UP CHRISTMAS LIST

Words and Music by DAVID FOSTER
and LINDA THOMPSON-JENNER

not a child_ but my heart still can dream. So here's my life - long wish, my
some-thing love - ly wrapped be - neath our tree. Well, heav - en sure - ly knows that

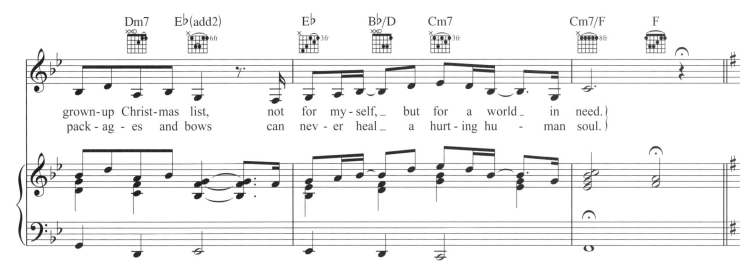

grown-up Christ-mas list, not for my - self,_ but for a world_ in need.
pack - ag - es and bows can nev - er heal_ a hurt-ing hu - man soul.

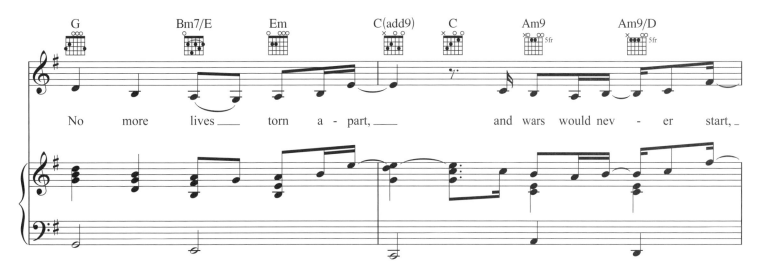

No more lives ___ torn a - part, ___ and wars would nev - er start, _

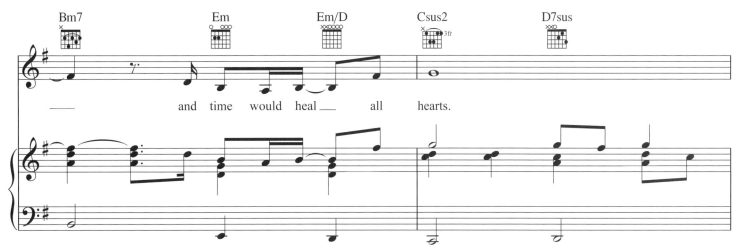

___ and time would heal ___ all hearts.

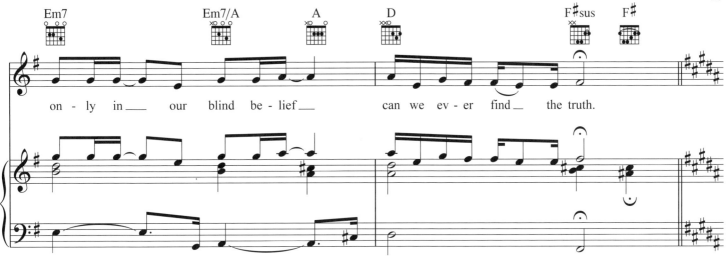

on - ly in ___ our blind be - lief ___ can we ev - er find ___ the truth.

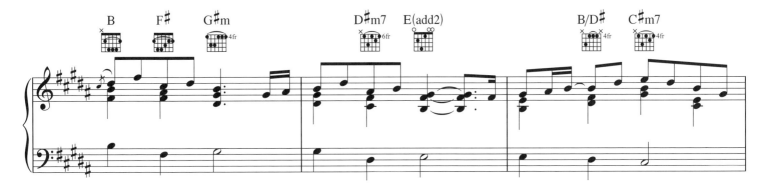

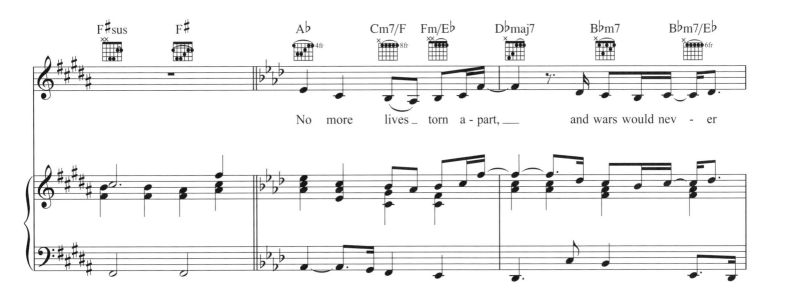

No more lives ___ torn a - part, ___ and wars would nev - er

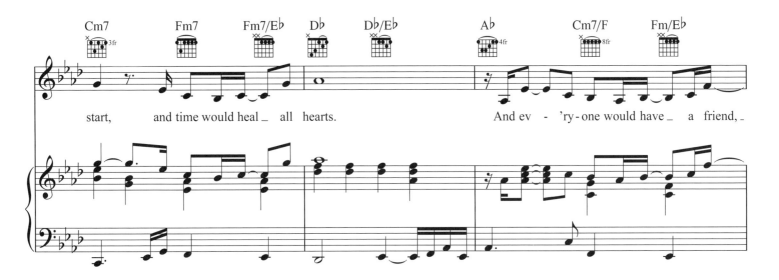

start, and time would heal ___ all hearts. And ev - 'ry - one would have ___ a friend, ___

MARY, DID YOU KNOW?

Words and Music by MARK LOWRY
and BUDDY GREENE

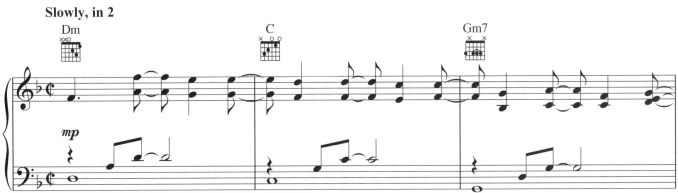

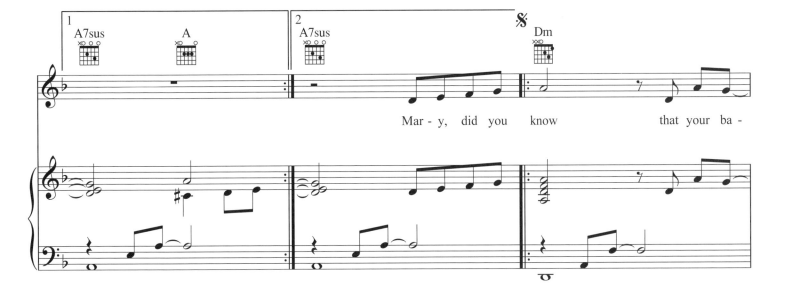

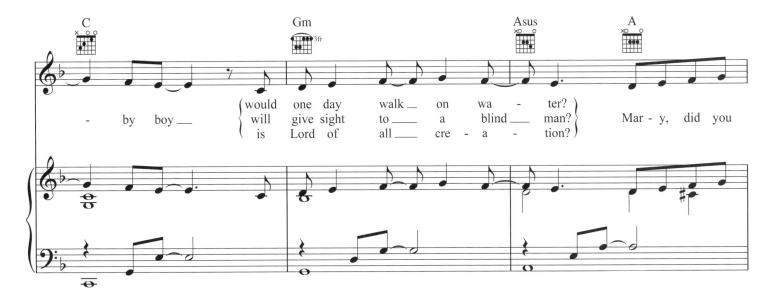

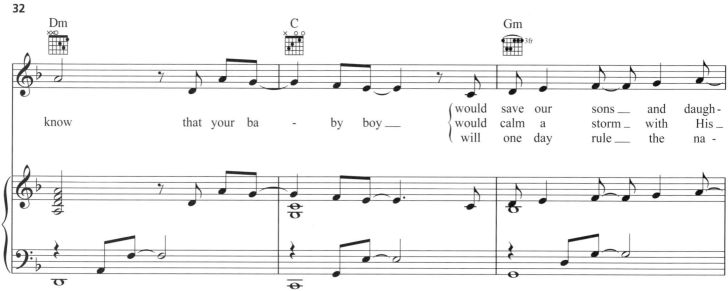

would save our sons __ and daugh-
would calm a storm __ with His __
will one day rule __ the na-

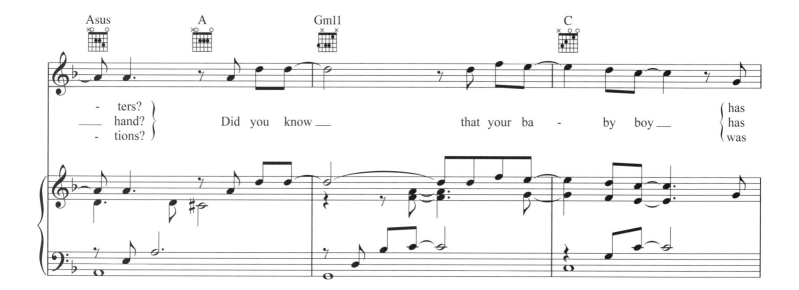

- ters?
__ hand?
- tions?

Did you know __ that your ba - by boy __ has
has
was

To Coda

come to make __ you new? __ This child __ that you __ de - liv-
walked where an - gels trod, __ and when you kissed your lit - tle ba-
heav - en's per - fect Lamb, __ and the sleep - ing Child __ you're hold-

-ered will soon de-liv-er you. ___
-by, you've kissed the face ___ of God? ___

___ Mar-y, did you ___ Oh, Mar-y, did you

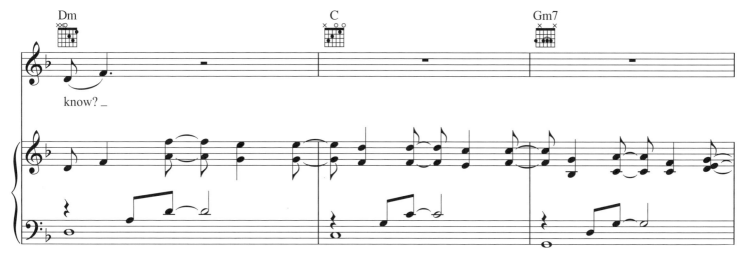

know? _

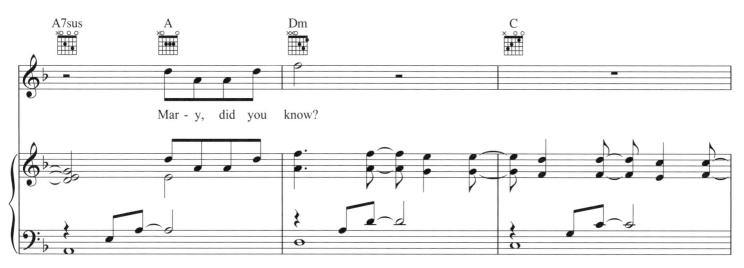

Mar-y, did you know?

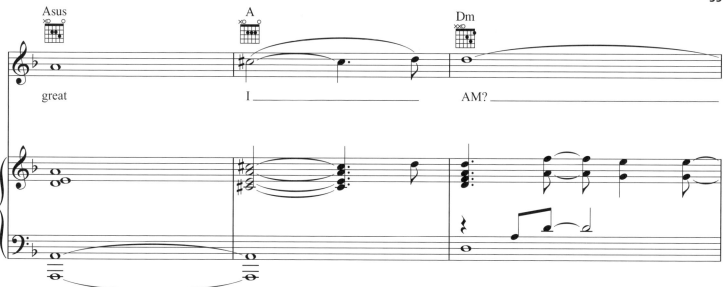

great

I _____ AM? _____

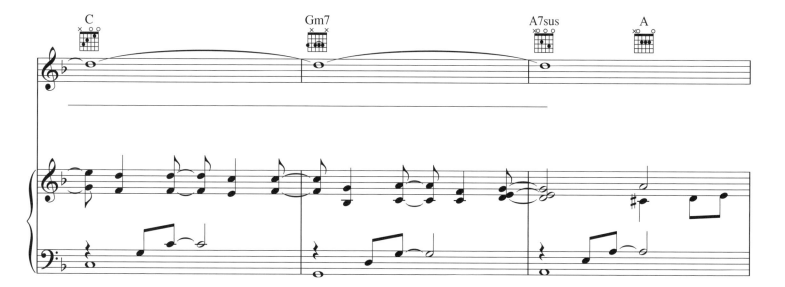

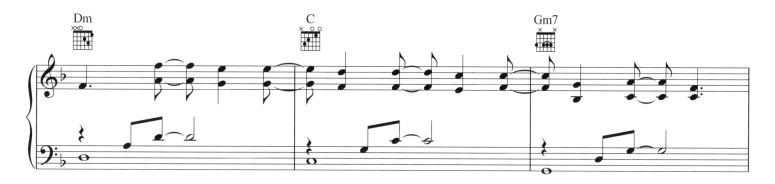

Freely

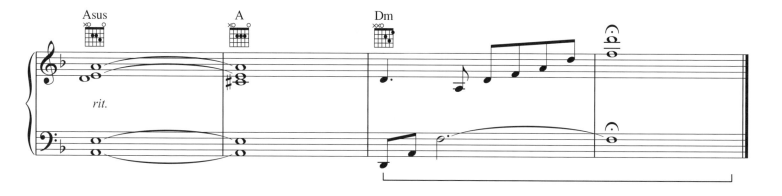

rit.

HAPPY XMAS
(War Is Over)

Written by JOHN LENNON
and YOKO ONO

38

Year. Let's hope it's a good one _____ with-out an - y

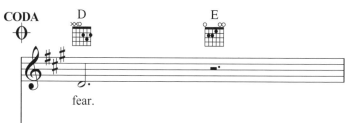

D.S. al Coda

fear. And so this is

CODA

fear.

War is o - ver if you want it;

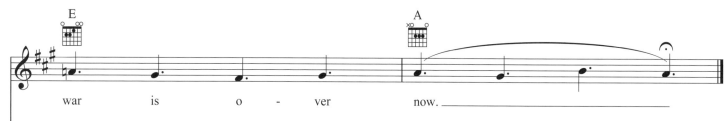

war is o - ver now. _____

IT MUST HAVE BEEN THE MISTLETOE
(Our First Christmas)

Words and Music by JUSTIN WILDE
and DOUG KONECKY

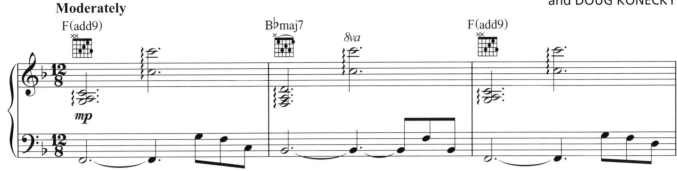

It must have been ___ the mis-tle-toe, ___ the

la-zy fire, ___ the fall-ing snow, the mag-ic in ___ the frost-y air, ___ that

feel-ing ev-'ry-where. It must have been ___ the pret-ty lights ___ that

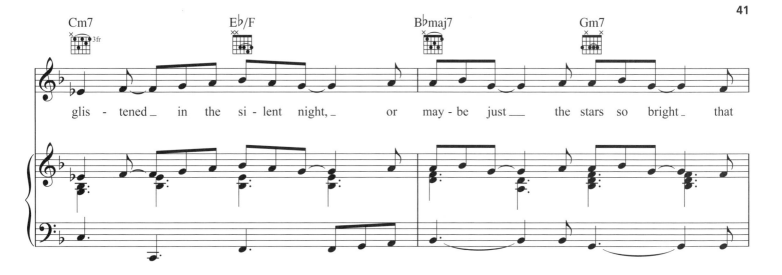

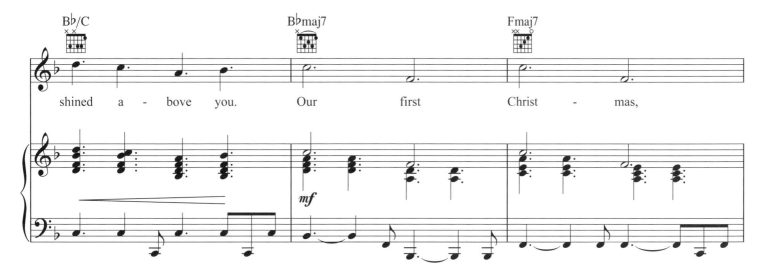

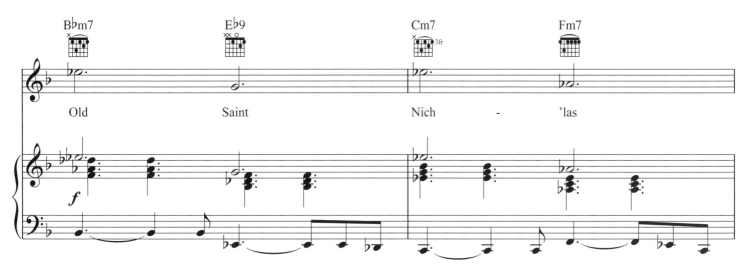

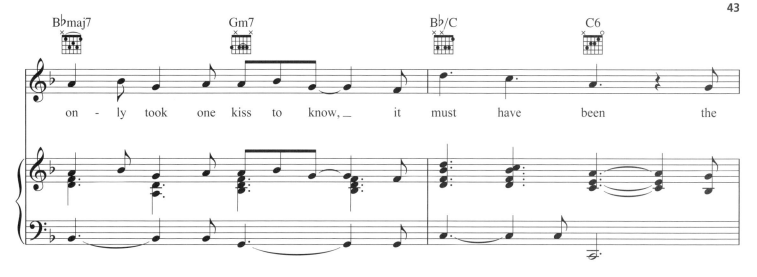

on - ly took one kiss to know, _ it must have been the

mis-tle-toe. Our first Christ - mas,

more than __ we'd been dream - ing of. _____

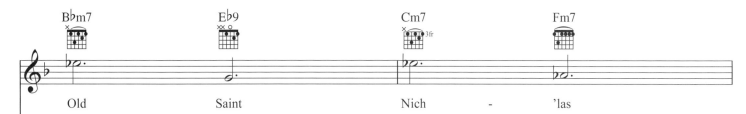

Old Saint Nich - 'las

44

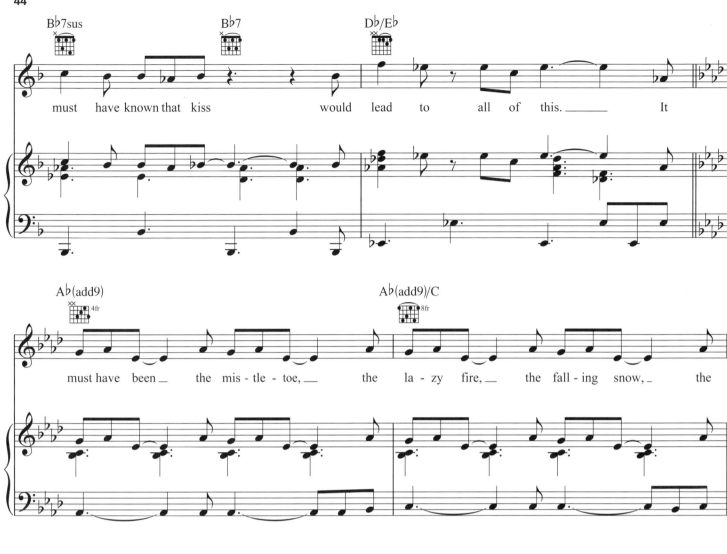

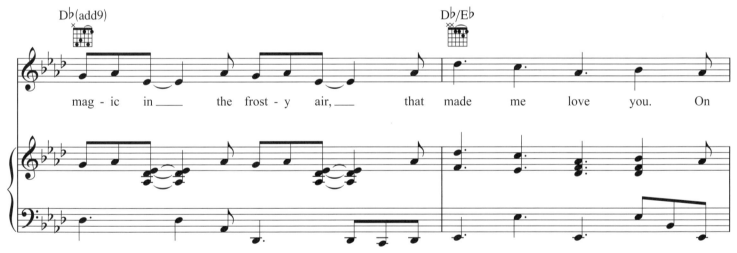

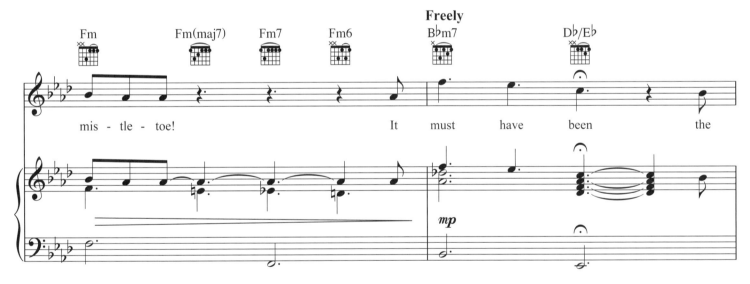

LITTLE SAINT NICK

Words and Music by BRIAN WILSON
and MIKE LOVE

Moderately fast

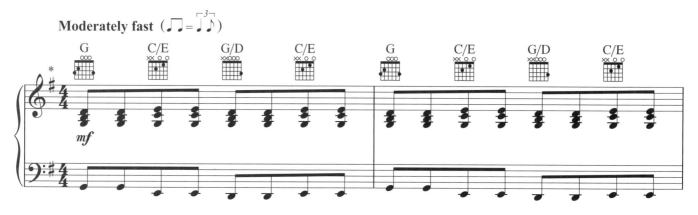

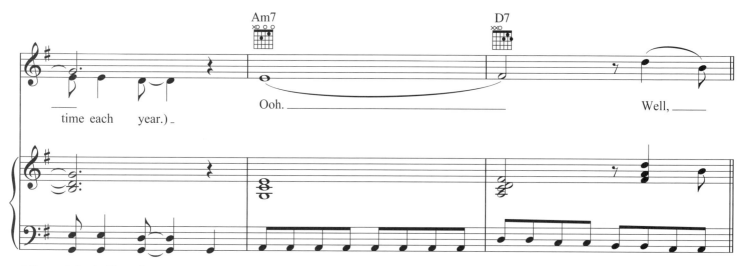

* Recorded a half step lower.

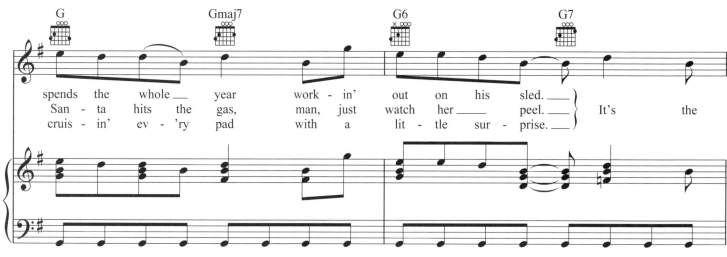

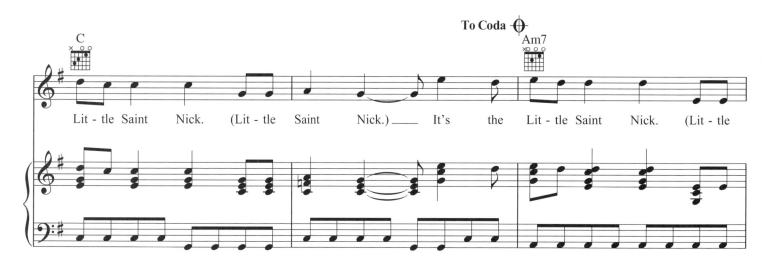

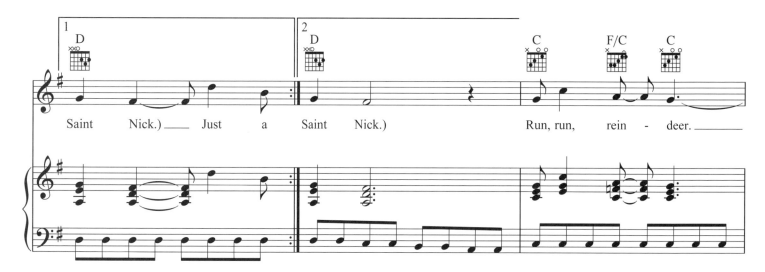

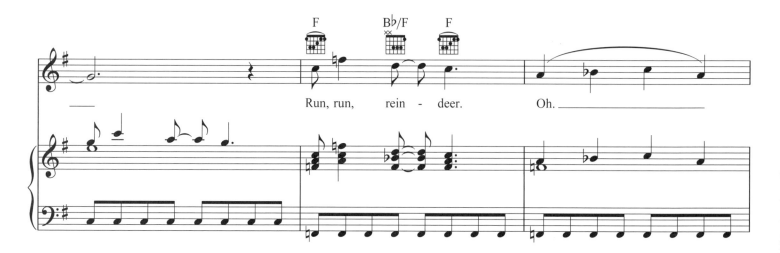

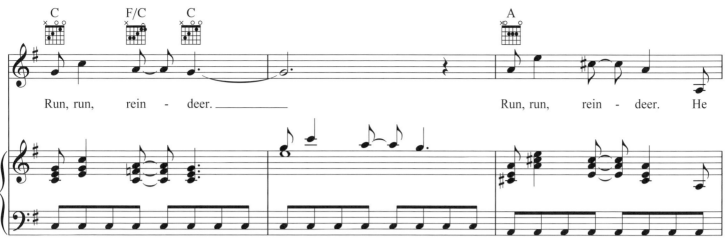

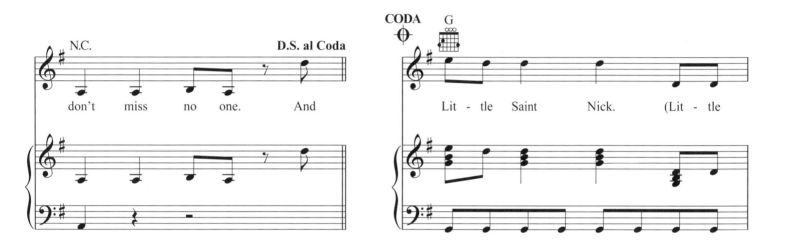

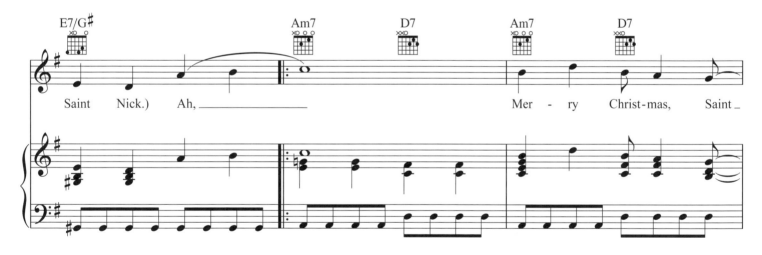

MISTER SANTA

Words and Music by
PAT BALLARD

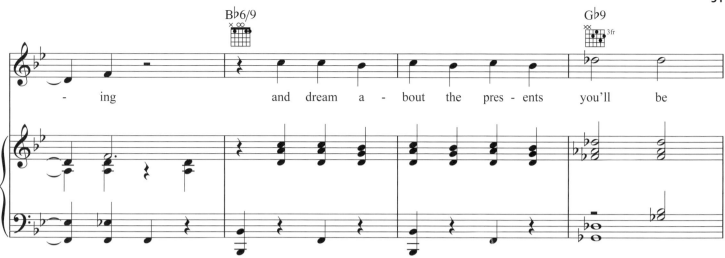

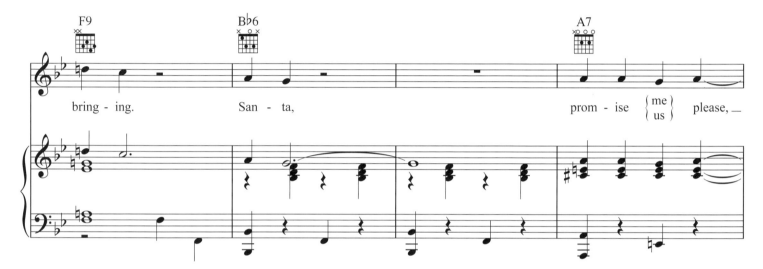

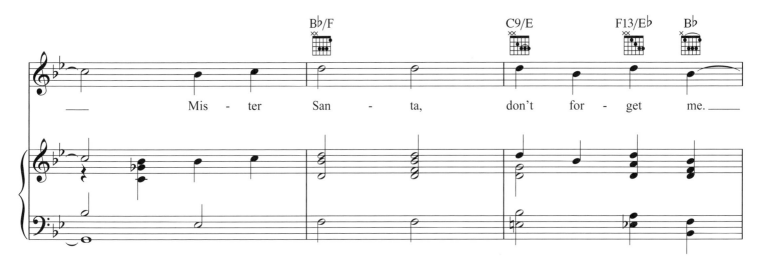

Additional Lyrics

2. Mister Santa, dear old Saint Nick,
Be awful careful and please don't get sick.
Put on your coat when breezes are blowin',
And when you cross the street look where you're goin'.
Santa, we (I) love you so,
We (I) hope you never get lost in the snow.
Take your time when you unpack,
Mister Santa, don't hurry back.

3. Mister Santa, we've been so good;
We've washed the dishes and done what we should.
Made up the beds and scrubbed up our toesies,
We've used a kleenex when we've blown our nosesies.
Santa, look at our ears, they're clean as whistles,
We're sharper than shears.
Now we've put you on the spot,
Mister Santa, bring us a lot.

MERRY CHRISTMAS, DARLING

Words and Music by RICHARD CARPENTER
and FRANK POOLER

54

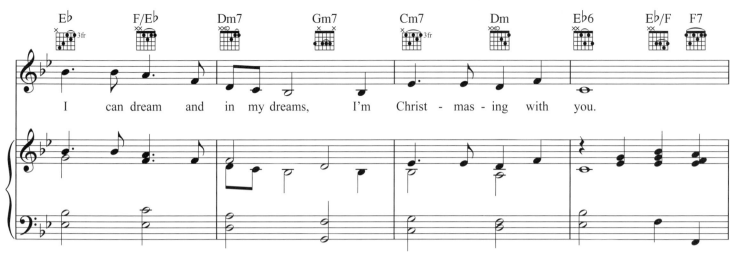

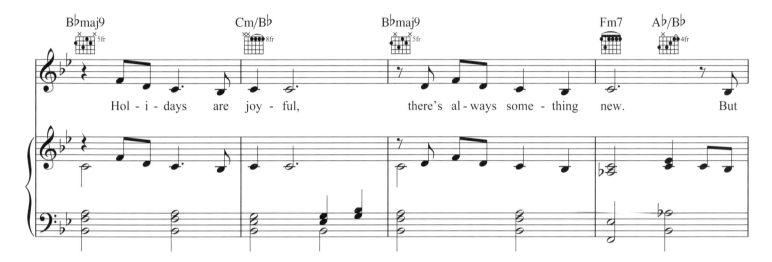

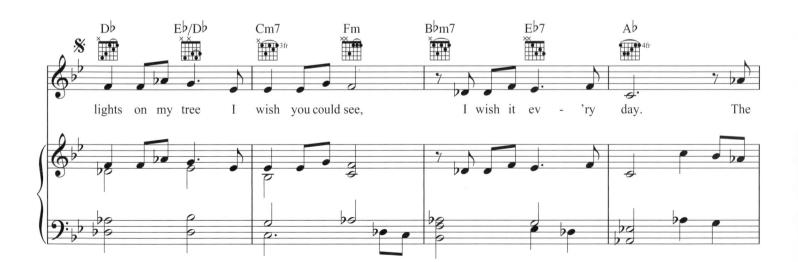

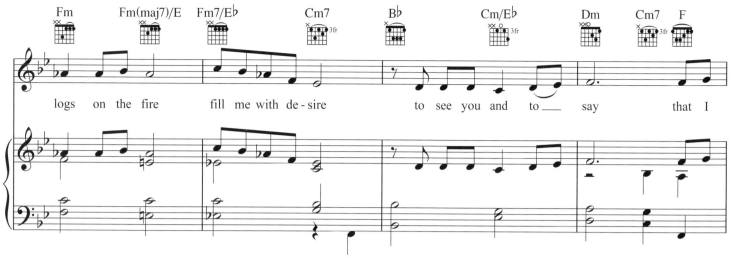

logs on the fire   fill me with de - sire   to see you and to ___ say   that I

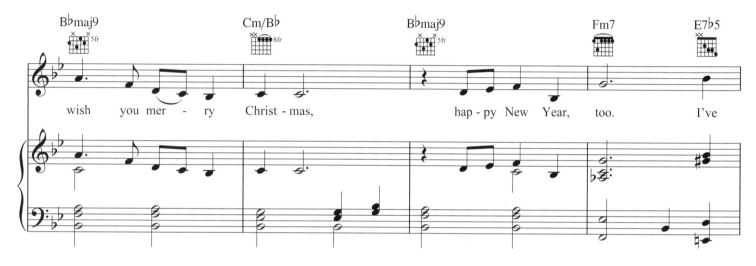

wish you mer - ry Christ - mas,   hap - py New Year, too.   I've

just one wish on this Christ - mas Eve: I wish I were with you.   The ___

I wish I were with you,   I wish I were with you. ___

RIVER

Words and Music by
JONI MITCHELL

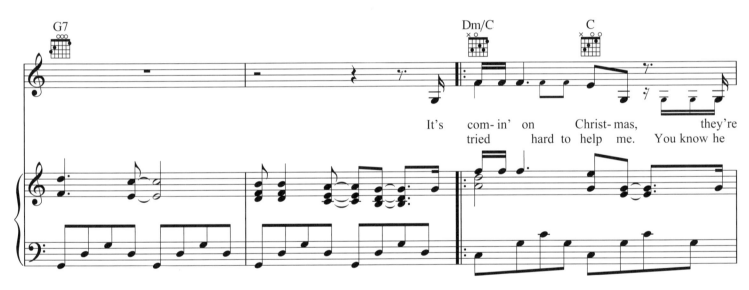

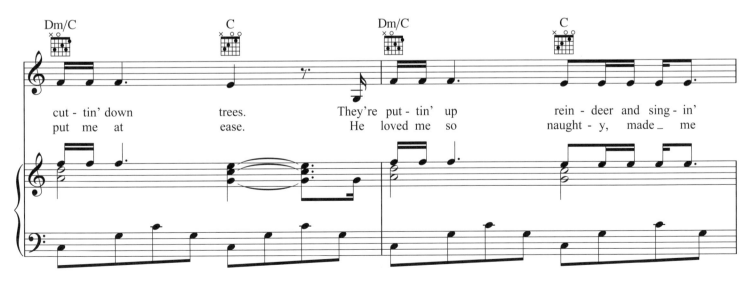

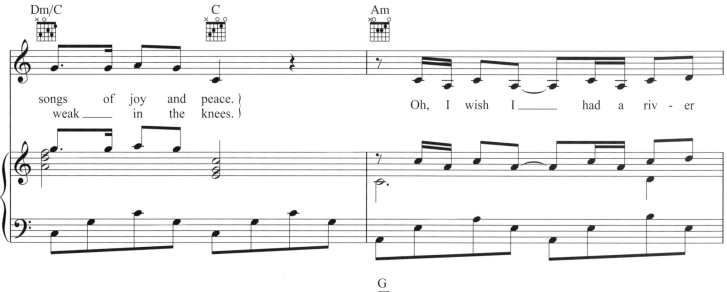

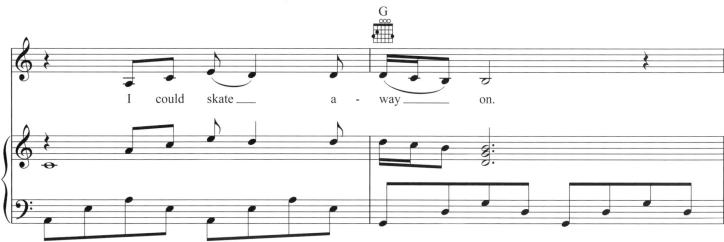

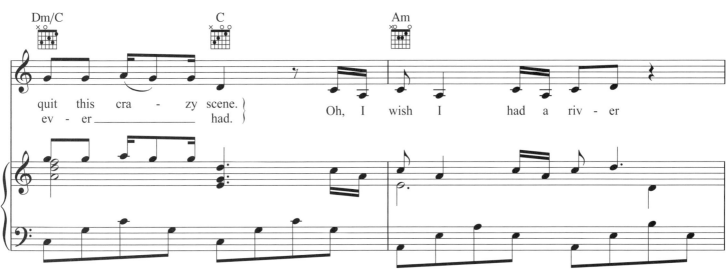

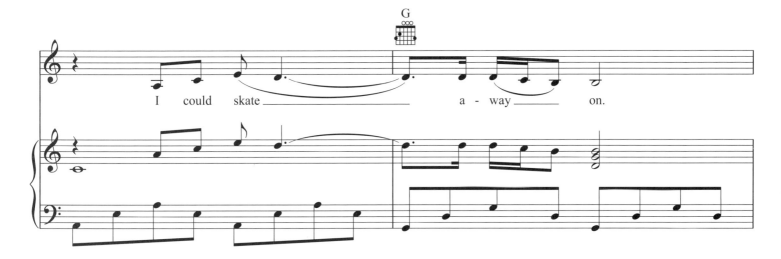

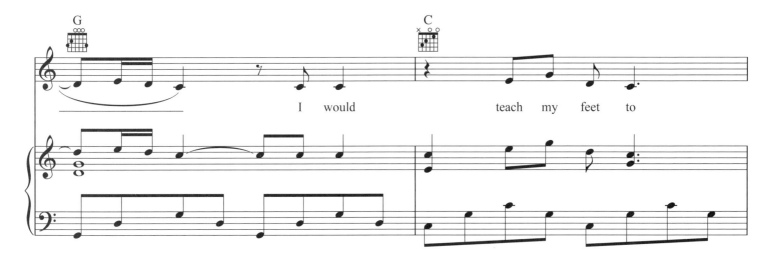

To Next Strain

60

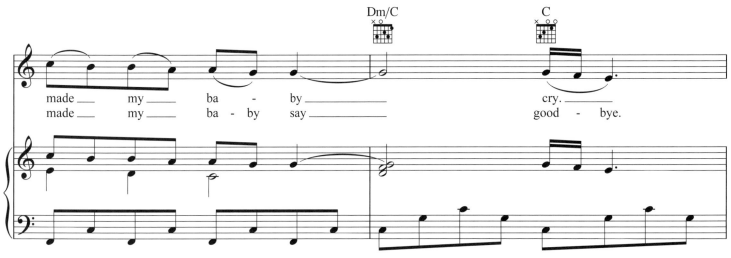

made ___ my ___ ba - by _____ cry. _____
made ___ my ___ ba - by say _____ good - bye.

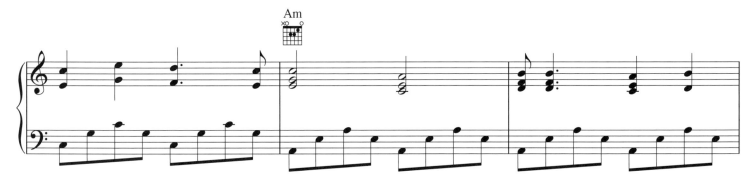

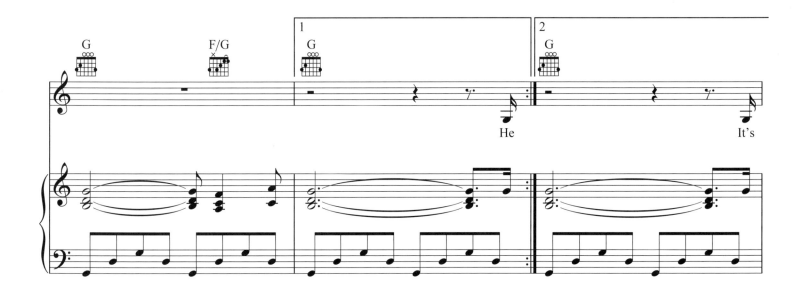

He   It's

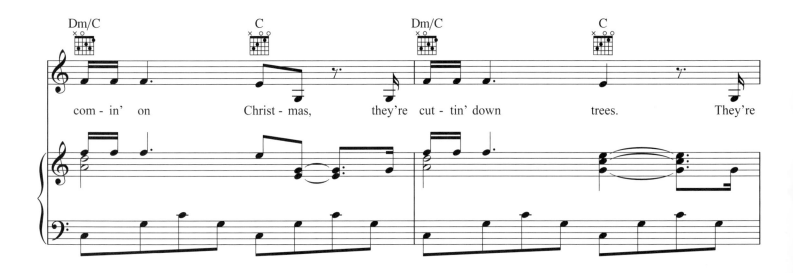

com - in' on   Christ - mas,   they're cut - tin' down   trees.   They're

put - tin' up rein - deer and sing - in' songs of joy and peace.

Oh I wish I____ had a riv - er I could skate ____ a -

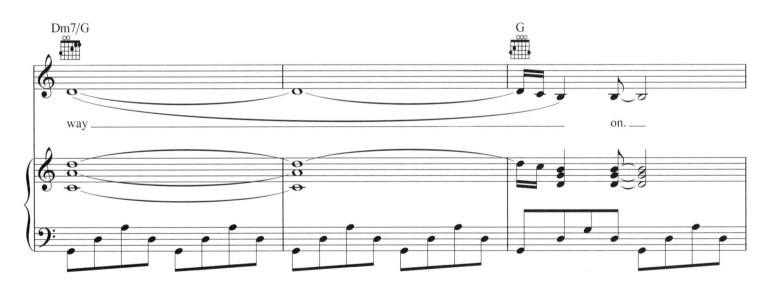

way _____ on. ___

SNOWFALL

Lyrics by RUTH THORNHILL
Music by CLAUDE THORNHILL

Moderately slow

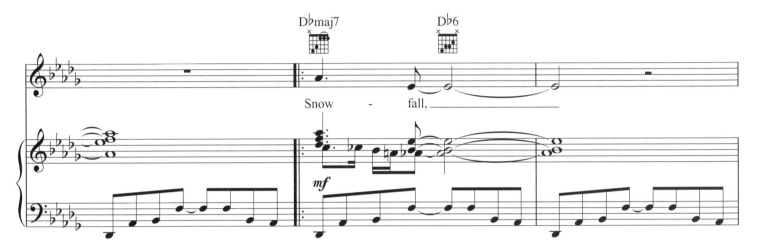

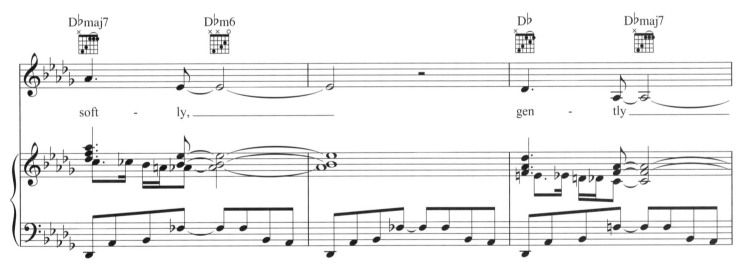

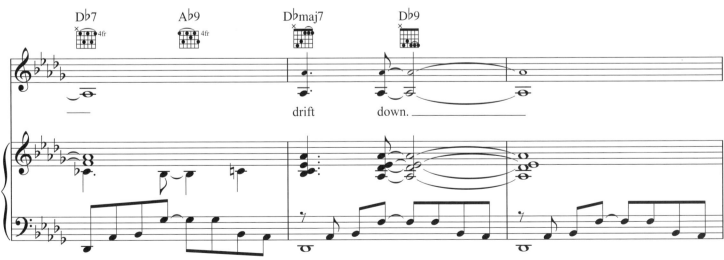

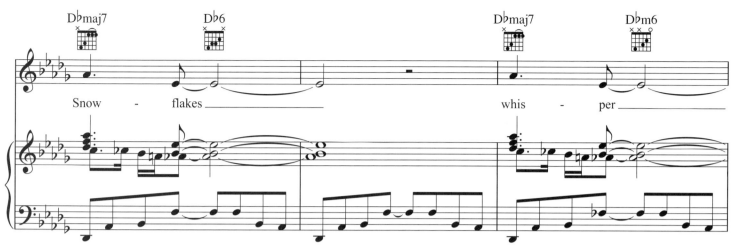

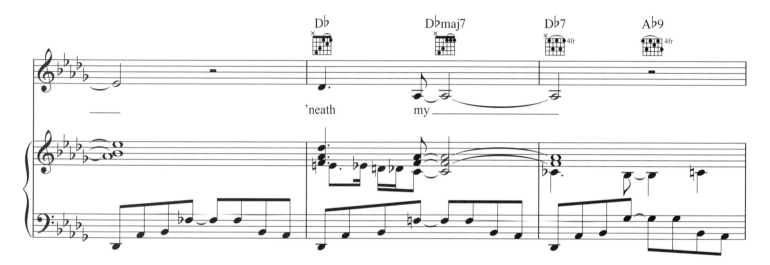

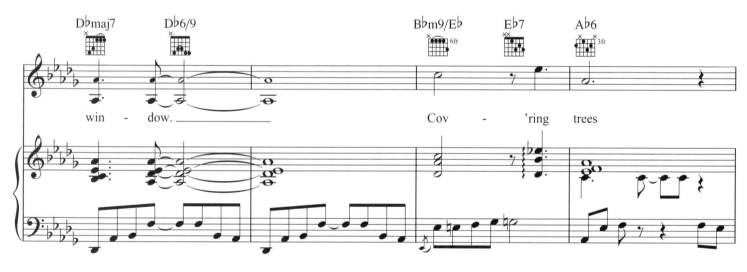

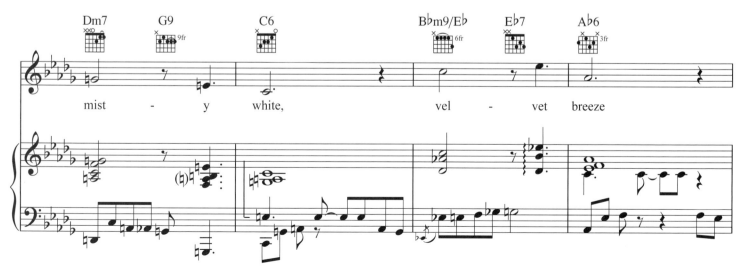

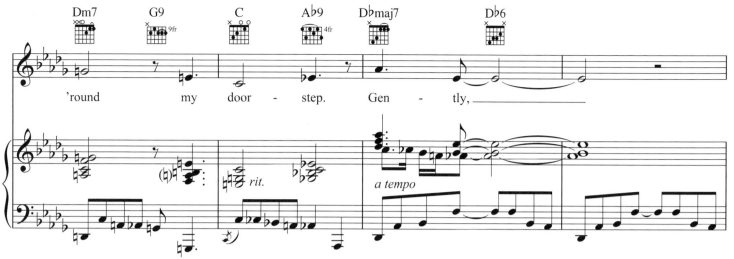

'round my door-step. Gen - tly, _____

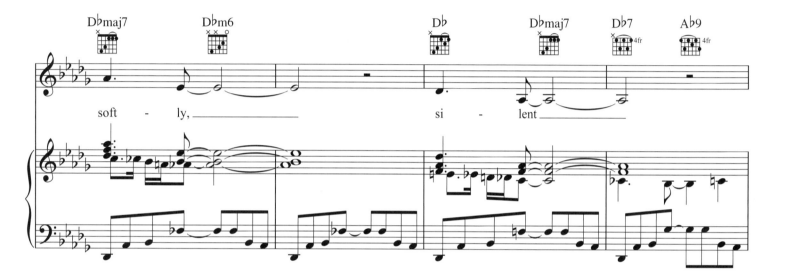

soft - ly, _____ si - lent _____

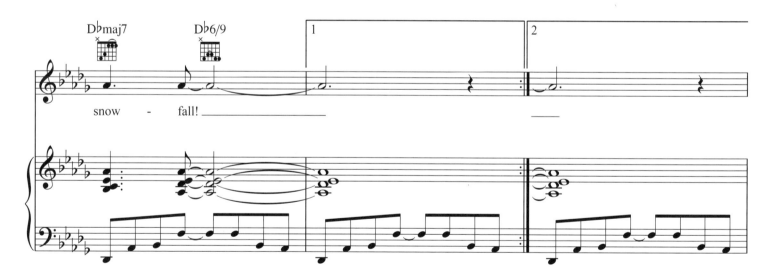

snow - fall! _____

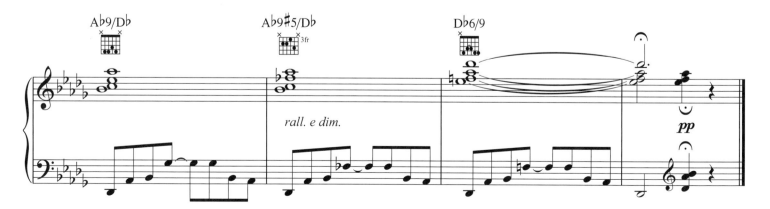

SANTA BABY

By JOAN JAVITS,
PHIL SPRINGER and TONY SPRINGER

Mis-ter "Claus," I feel as though I know ya, _____ so
you won't mind if I should get fa-mil-ya, will ya?

San-ta Ba-by, just slip a sa-ble un-der the tree _____
San-ta Ba-by, one lit-tle thing I real-ly do need; _____

SOMEDAY AT CHRISTMAS

Words and Music by RONALD N. MILLER
and BRYAN WELLS

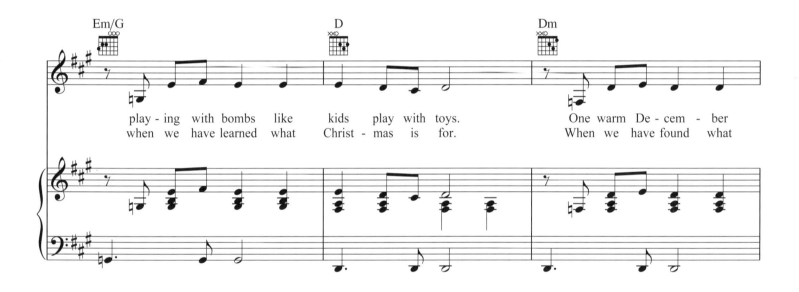

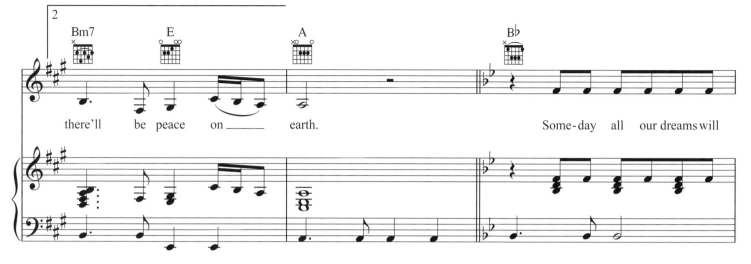

there'll be peace on _____ earth. Some-day all our dreams will

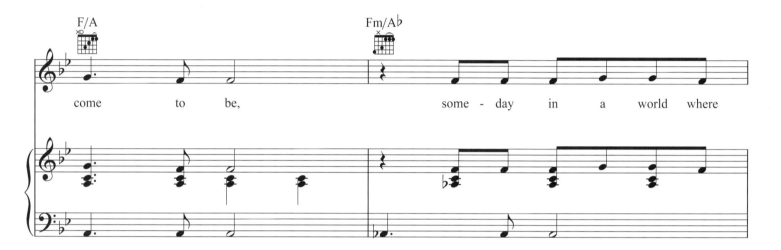

come to be, some - day in a world where

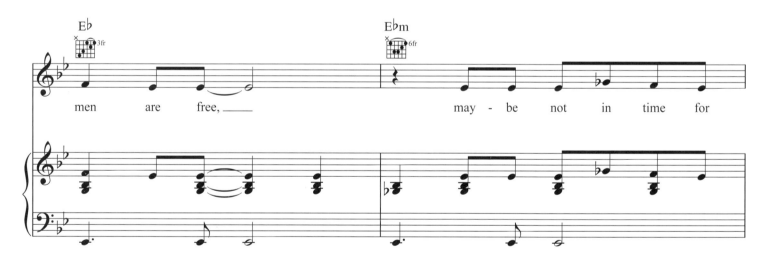

men are free, _____ may - be not in time for

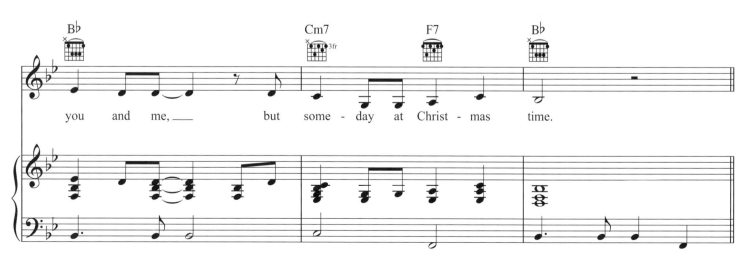

you and me, _____ but some - day at Christ - mas time.

Some - day at Christ - mas we'll see a land with no hun - gry chil - dren,
Some - day at Christ - mas there'll be no tears when all men are e - qual and

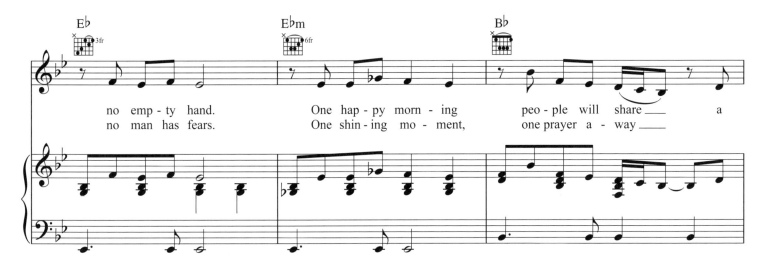

no emp - ty hand. One hap - py morn - ing peo - ple will share ___ a
no man has fears. One shin - ing mo - ment, one prayer a - way ___

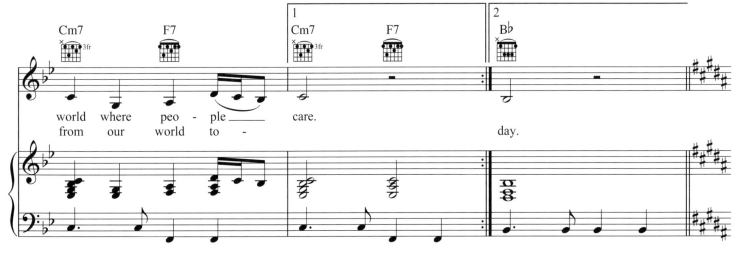

world where peo - ple ___ care.
from our world to - day.

Some - day all our dreams will come to be, ___ some - day in a world where

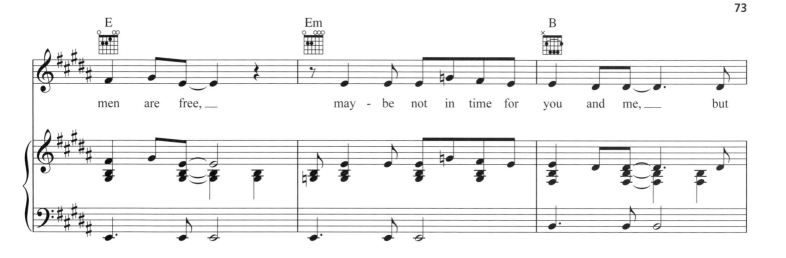

men are free, ___ may - be not in time for you and me, ___ but

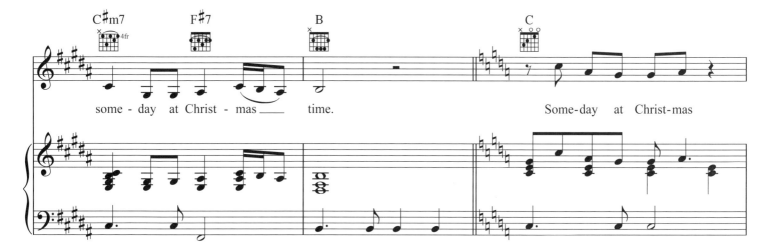

some - day at Christ - mas ___ time. Some - day at Christ - mas

man will not fail. Hate will be gone and love ___ will pre - vail.

Some - day a new world that we can start ___ with hope in ev - 'ry heart. ___

Some-day all our dreams will come to be,

some-day in a world where men are free, may-be not in time for

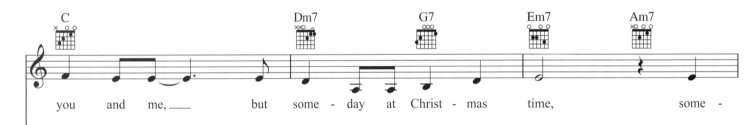

you and me,___ but some-day at Christ-mas time, some-

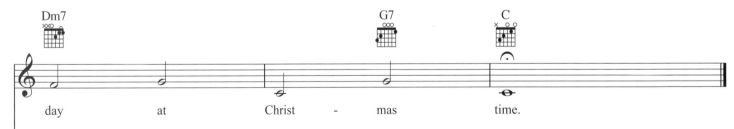

day at Christ - mas time.

UNDERNEATH THE TREE

Words and Music by KELLY CLARKSON
and GREG KURSTIN

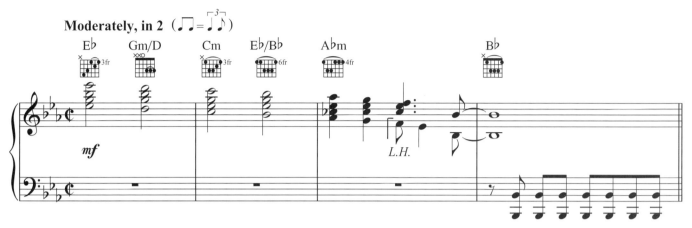

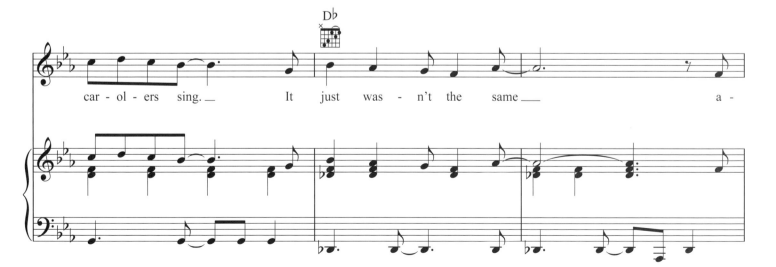

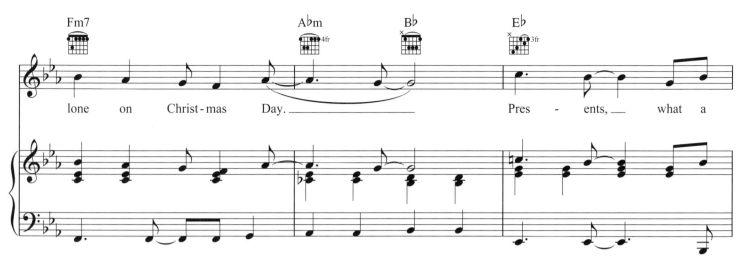

lone on Christ-mas Day. _____ Pres - ents, _ what a

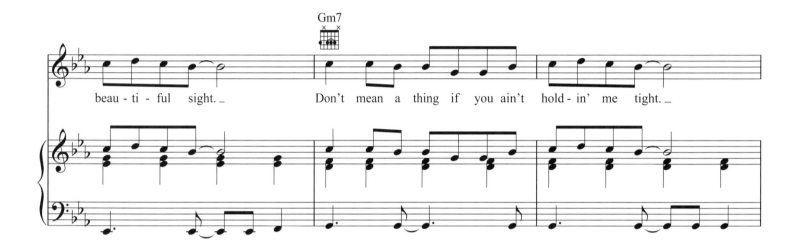

beau-ti-ful sight. _ Don't mean a thing if you ain't hold-in' me tight. _

You're all that I need ____ un-der-neath the tree. _

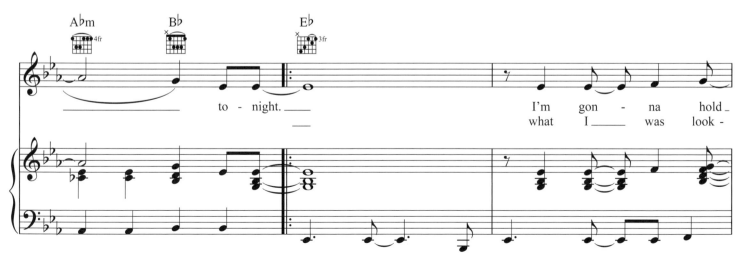

_____ to - night. ____ I'm gon - na hold _
___ what I ____ was look-

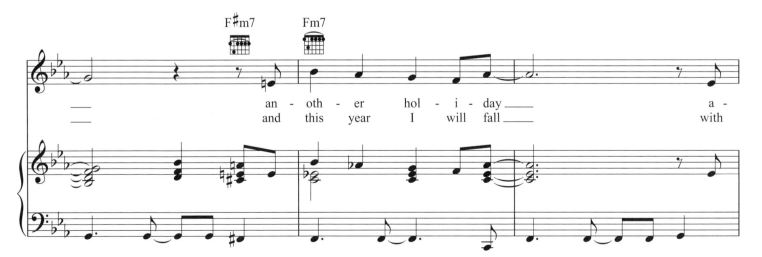

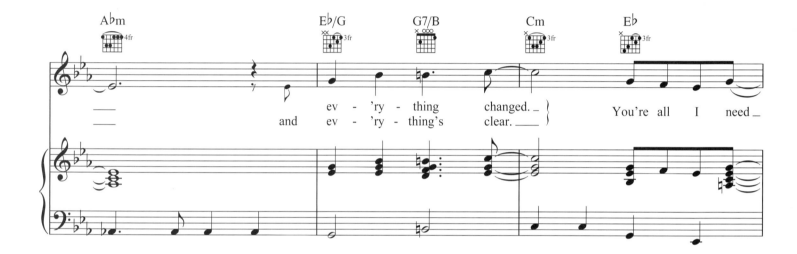

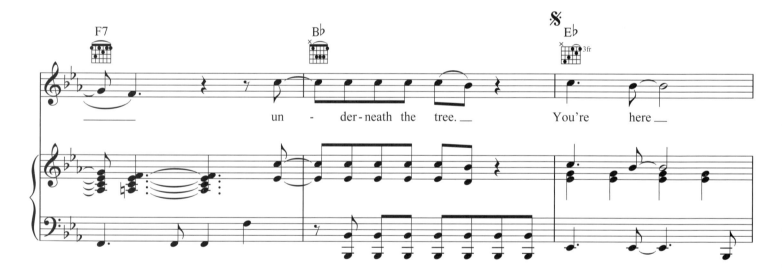

just was - n't the same ___ a - lone on Christ-mas Day. ___

___ Pres - ents, ___ what a beau - ti - ful sight. ___

Don't mean a thing if you ain't hold - in' me tight. ___ You're all that I need ___

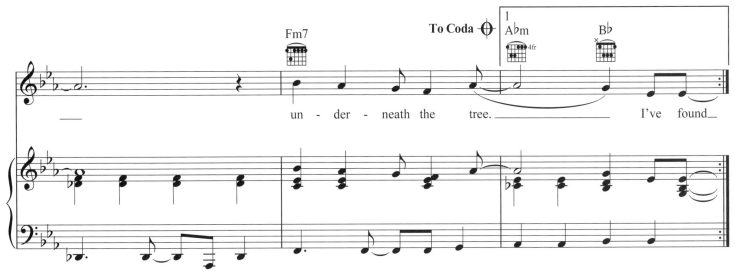

___ un - der - neath the tree. ___ I've found ___

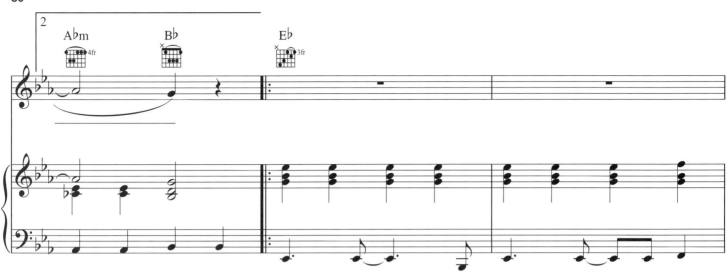

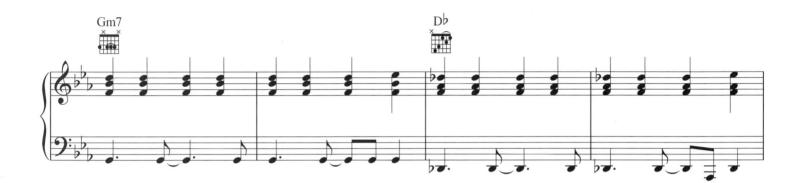

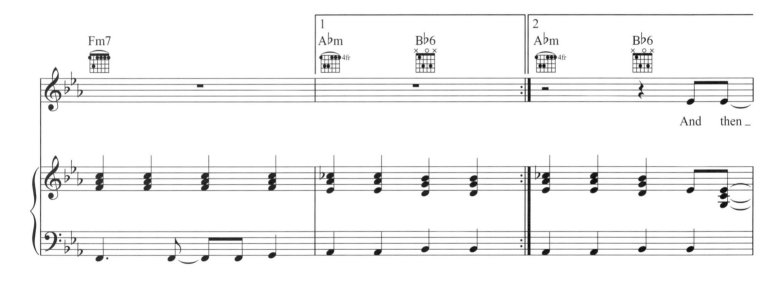

And then _

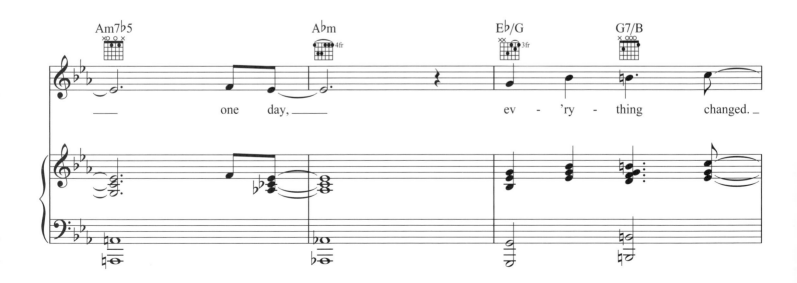

one day, _ ev - 'ry - thing changed. _

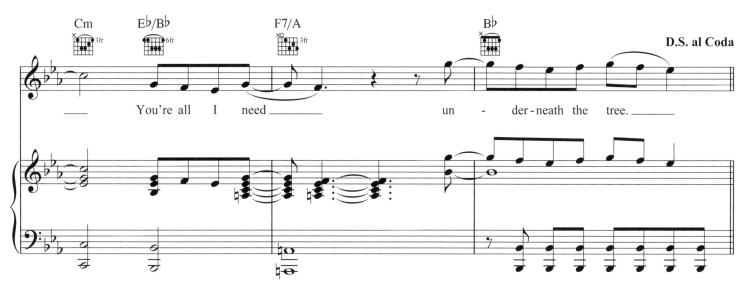

D.S. al Coda

You're all I need _____ un - der-neath the tree. _____

to - night. _____

Repeat and Fade | Optional Ending

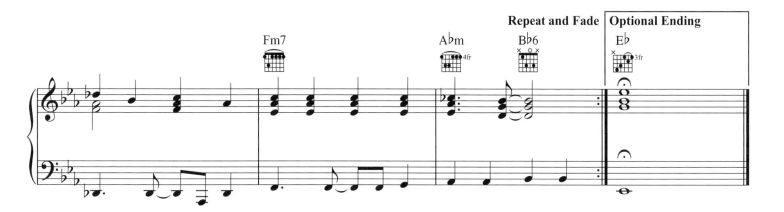

THAT SPIRIT OF CHRISTMAS

Words and Music by PARNELL DAVISON,
MABLE JOHN and JOEL WEBSTER

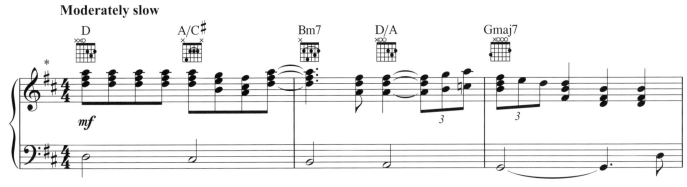

Moderately slow

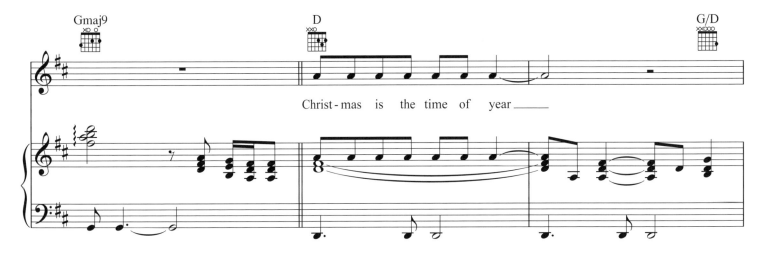

Christ-mas is the time of year _____

for be - ing with the ones we love.

Shar-ing so much joy _ and cheer. _

_____ What a won - der - ful feel - ing _____

watch - ing _ the ones

Recorded a half step lower.

we love hav-ing __ so much fun. __

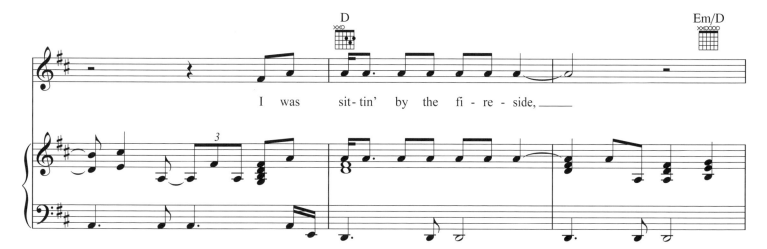

I was sit-tin' by the fi-re-side, __

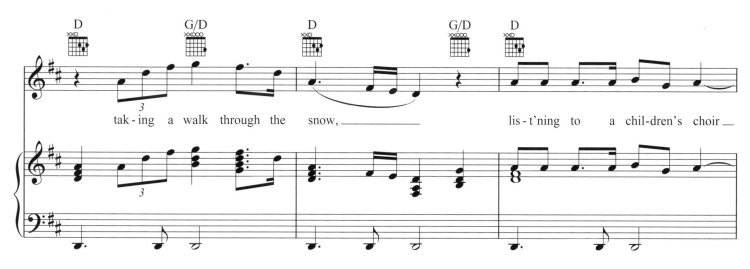

tak-ing a walk through the snow, __ lis-t'ning to a chil-dren's choir __

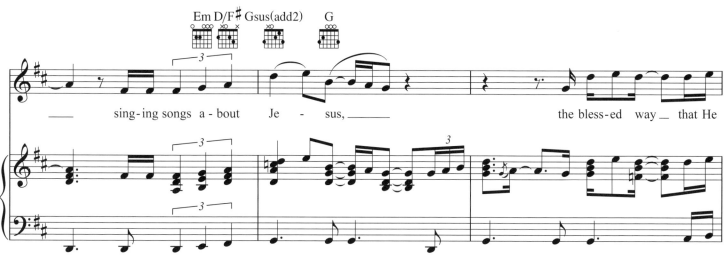

__ sing-ing songs a-bout Je - sus, __ the bless-ed way __ that He

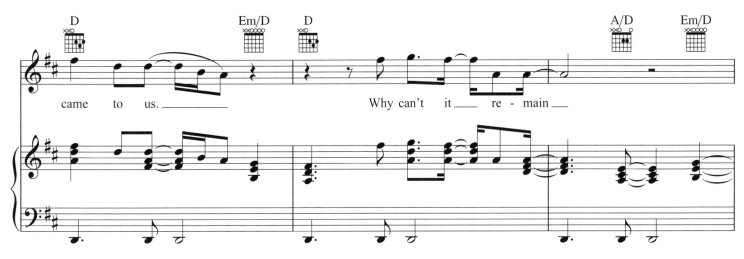

came to us. _____ Why can't it ___ re - main ___

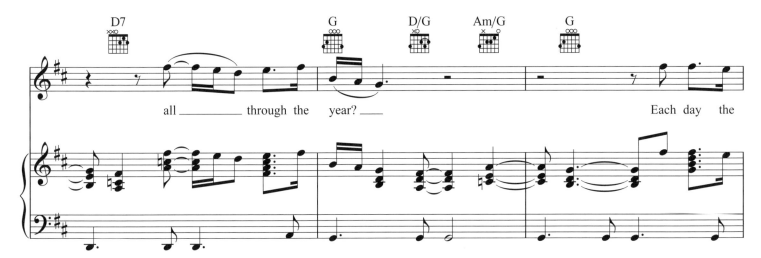

all _____ through the year? ___ Each day the

same, _____ ah, that's what I ___ wan-na hear. _____

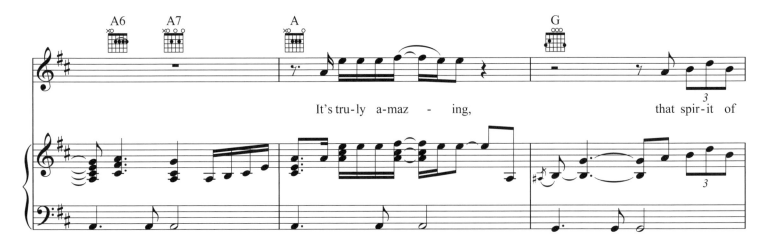

It's tru-ly a-maz - ing, that spir-it of

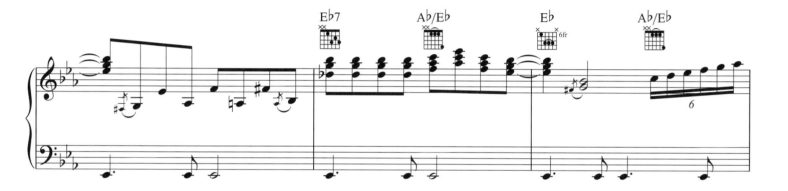

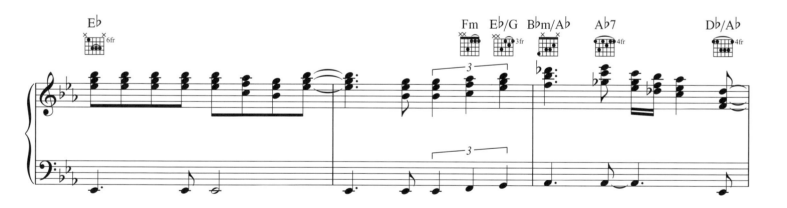

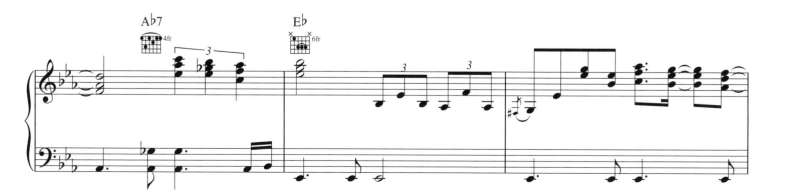

All the kin-folk gath-er ___ 'round ___

___ the love-ly Christ-mas ___ tree. ___

Hearts are glow-ing full of joy, ___ sense the gifts that we're giv - ing ___

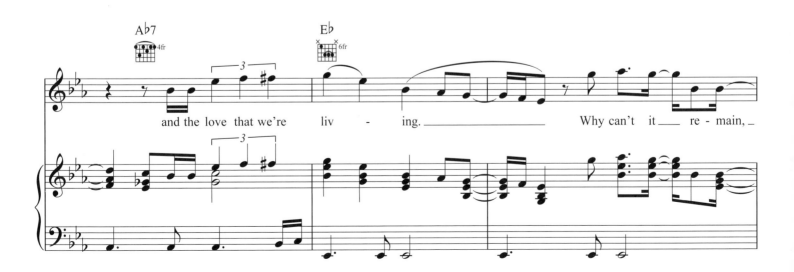

and the love that we're liv - ing. ___ Why can't it ___ re - main, ___

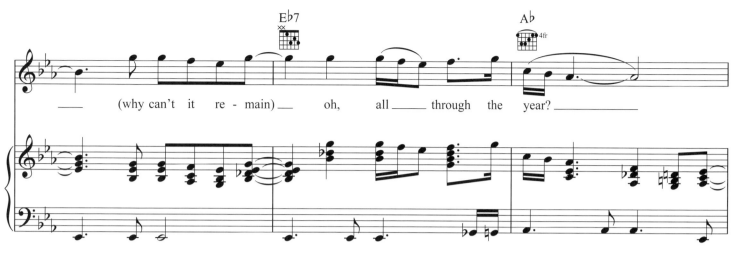

(why can't it re - main) __ oh, all __ through the year? __

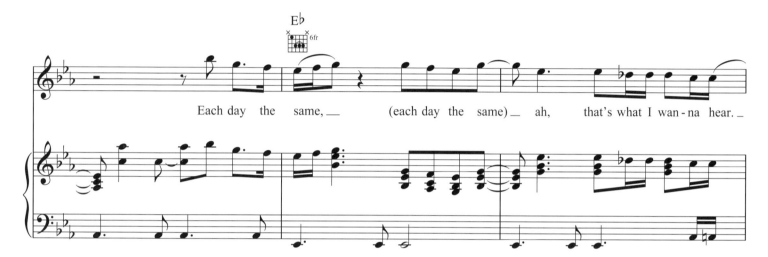

Each day the same, __ (each day the same) __ ah, that's what I wan-na hear. __

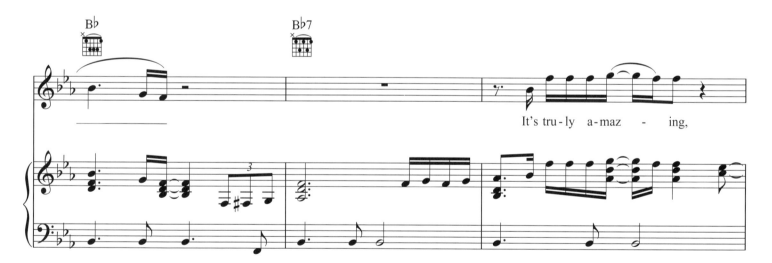

It's tru-ly a-maz - ing,

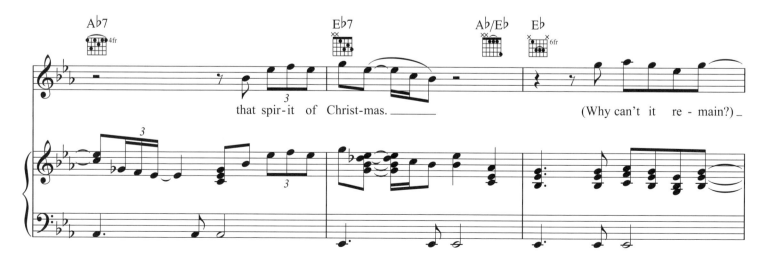

that spir-it of Christ-mas. __ (Why can't it re - main?) _

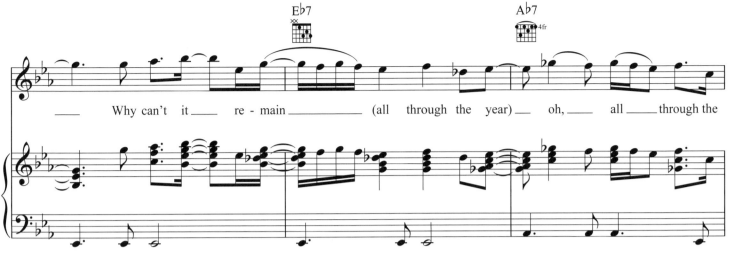

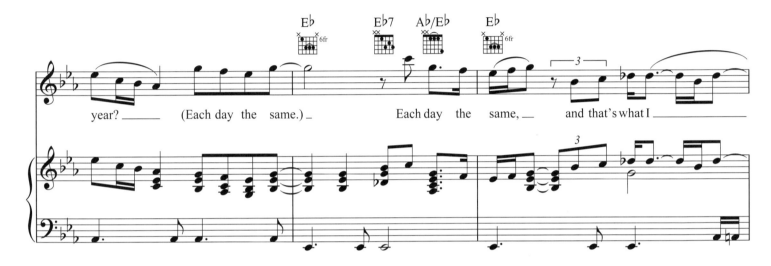

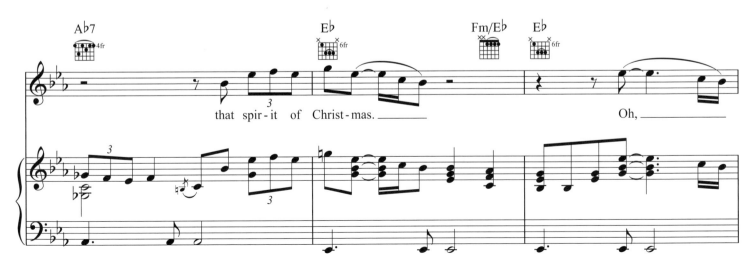

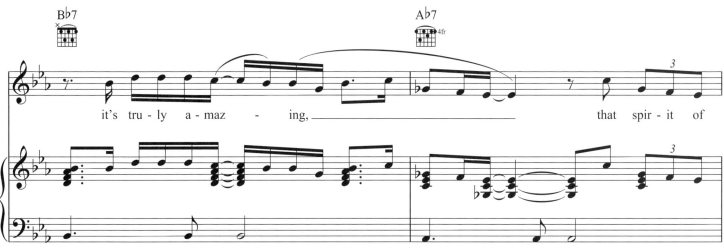

it's tru-ly a-maz - ing, _____ that spir-it of

Christ - mas. ___ Ain't it so? It's tru-ly a-

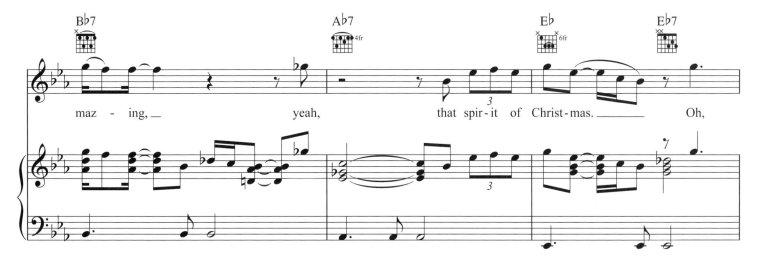

maz - ing, _ yeah, that spir-it of Christ-mas. _____ Oh,

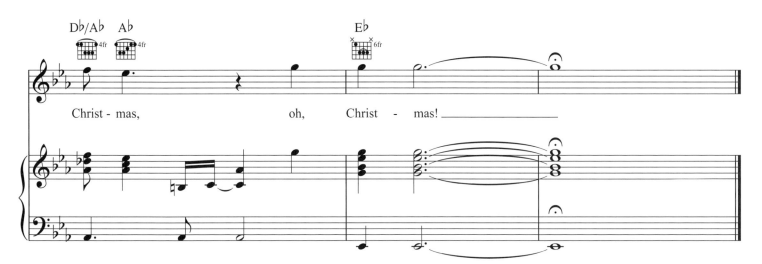

Christ - mas, oh, Christ - mas! _____

THIS CHRISTMAS

Words and Music by DONNY HATHAWAY
and NADINE McKINNOR

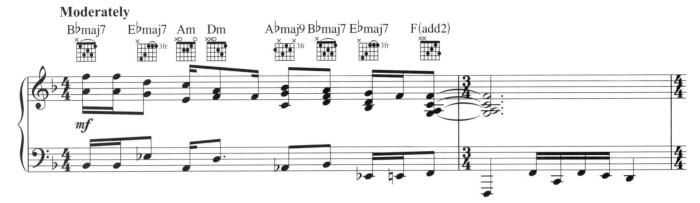

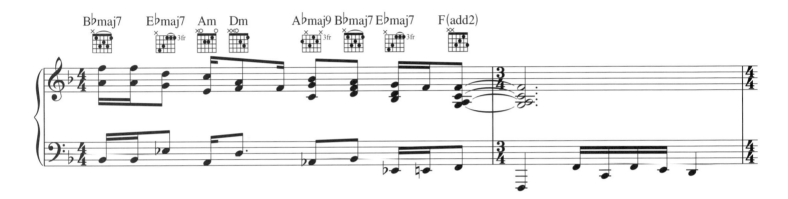

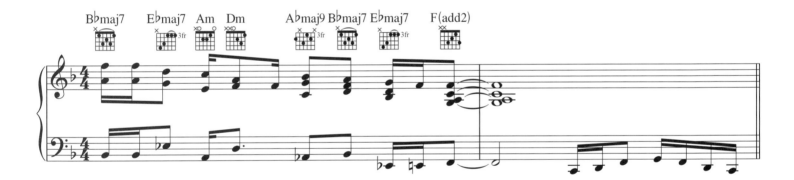

(1.,4.) Hang   all   the mis - tle - toe.__   I'm   gon - na get   to know you   bet - ter _____
(2.) Pres - ents   and cards are   here. __   My   world   is filled with cheer and   you, _____
(3.) *Piano solo ad lib.*

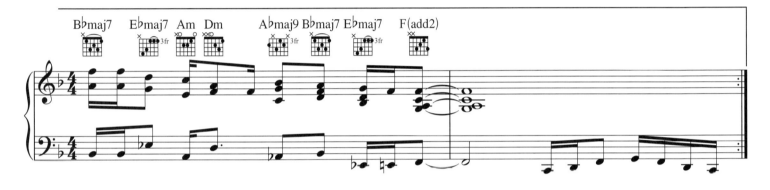

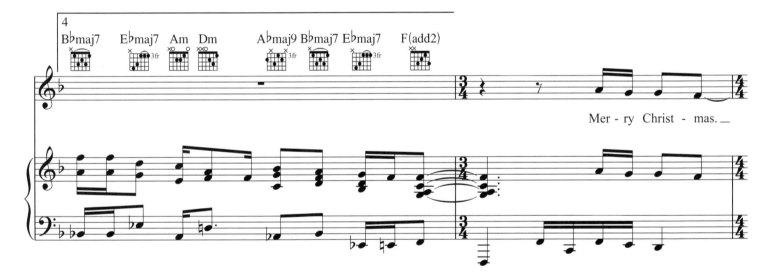

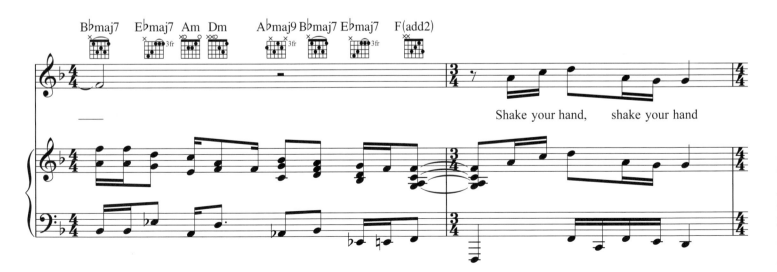

WHERE ARE YOU CHRISTMAS?

from DR. SEUSS' HOW THE GRINCH STOLE CHRISTMAS

Words and Music by WILL JENNINGS,
JAMES HORNER and MARIAH CAREY

Where are you, Christ - mas? Why can't I find you? Why have you gone a-

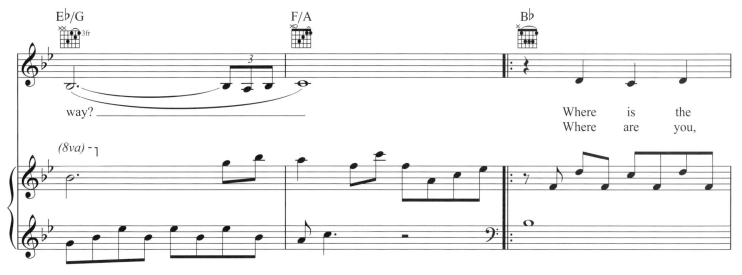

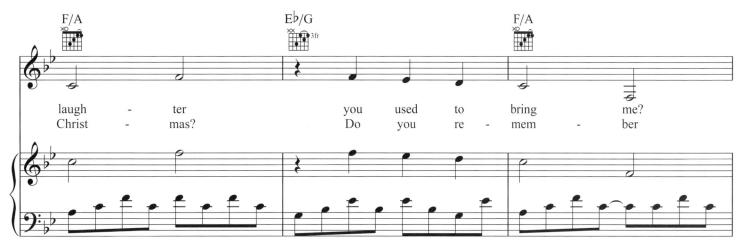

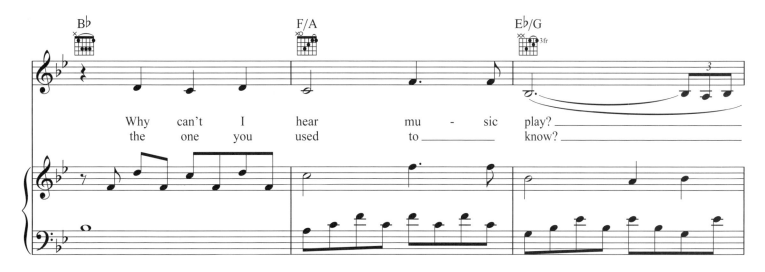

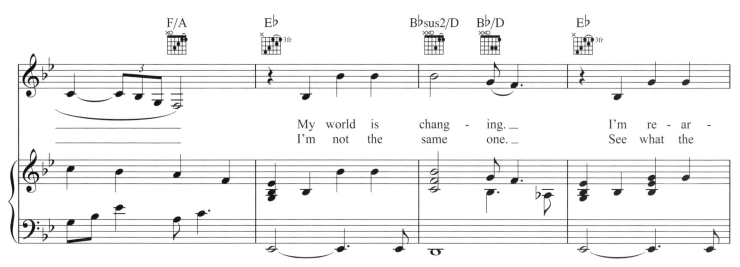

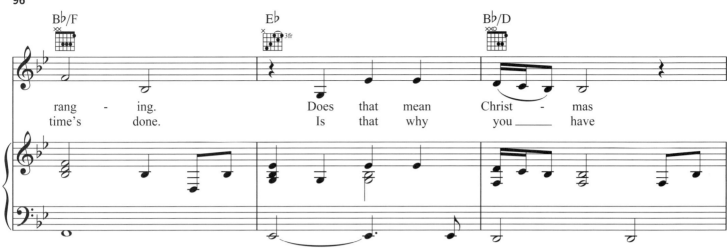

rang - ing.
time's done.
Does that mean Christ - mas
Is that why you _____ have

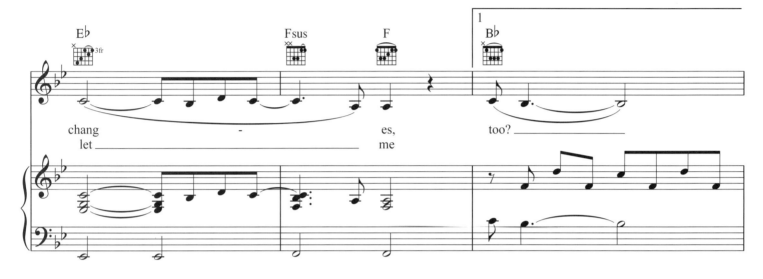

chang - es, too? _____
let _____ me

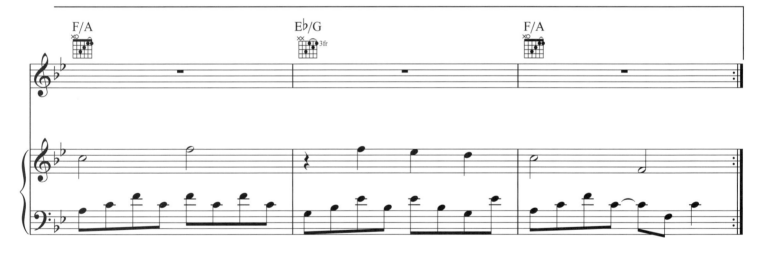

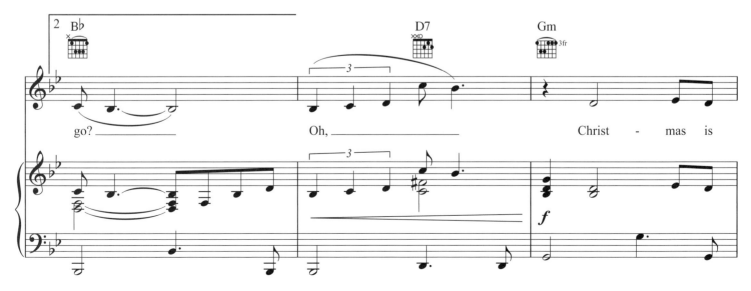

go? _____ Oh, _____ Christ - mas is

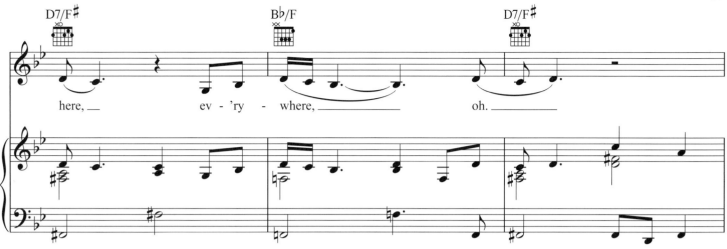

here, __ ev - 'ry - where, _____ oh. _____

Christ - mas is here, __ if you care. _____

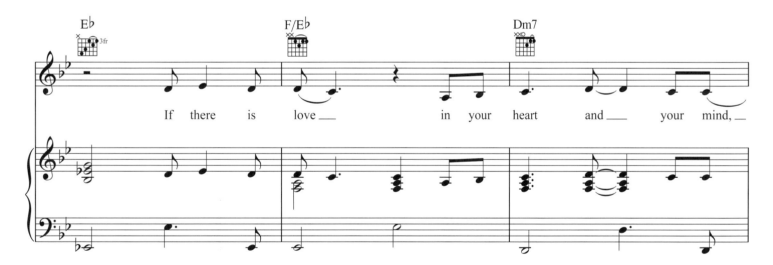

If there is love ___ in your heart and ___ your mind, __

you will feel like Christ - mas all the

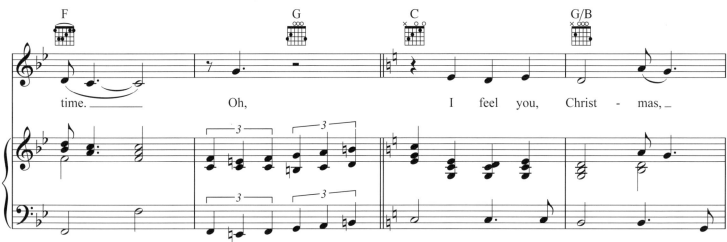

time. _____ Oh, I feel you, Christ-mas, _

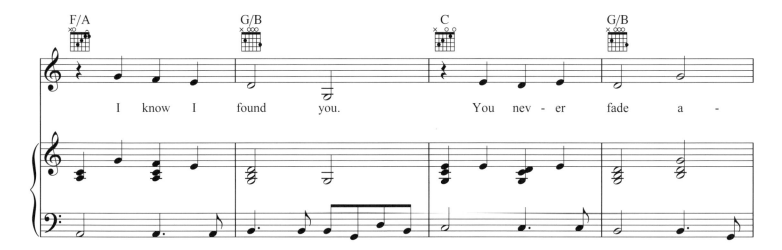

I know I found you. You nev-er fade a-

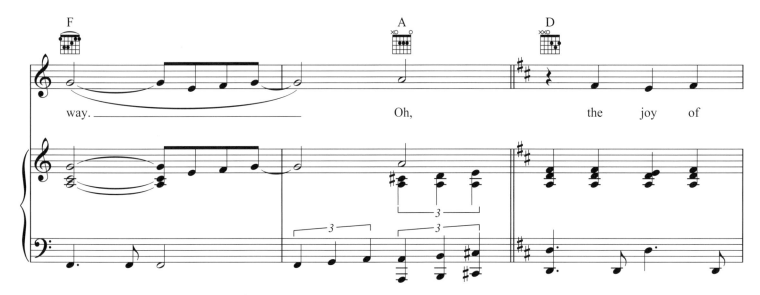

way. _____ Oh, the joy of

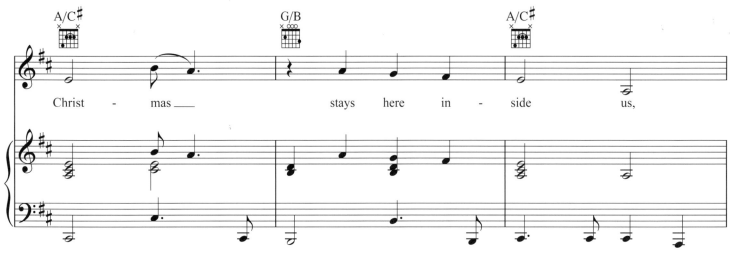

Christ-mas _____ stays here in-side us,

fills each and ev - 'ry heart _____ with love. _____

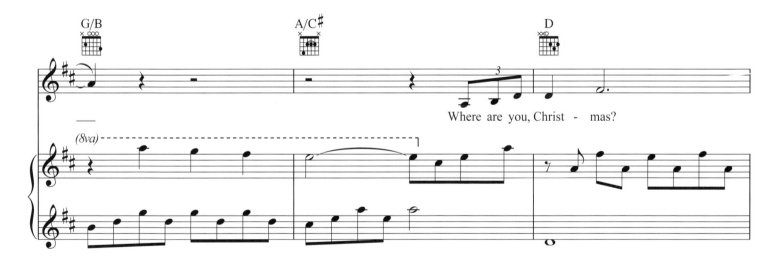

_____ Where are you, Christ - mas?

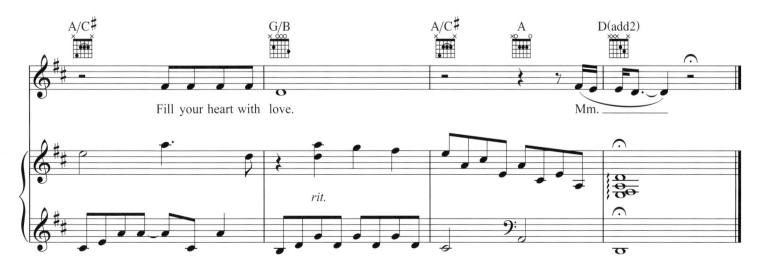

Fill your heart with love. Mm. _____

WONDERFUL CHRISTMASTIME

Words and Music by
PAUL McCARTNEY

Sim - ply hav - ing a won - der - ful Christ - mas - time.

time. The choir of chil - dren

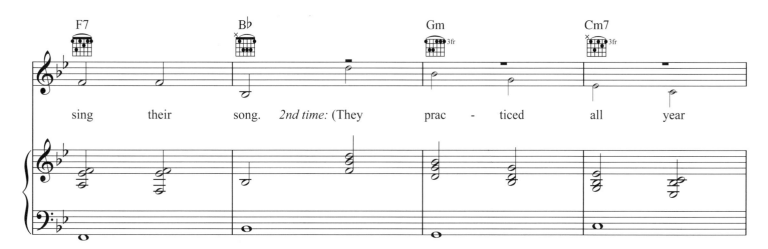

sing their song. *2nd time:* (They prac - ticed all year

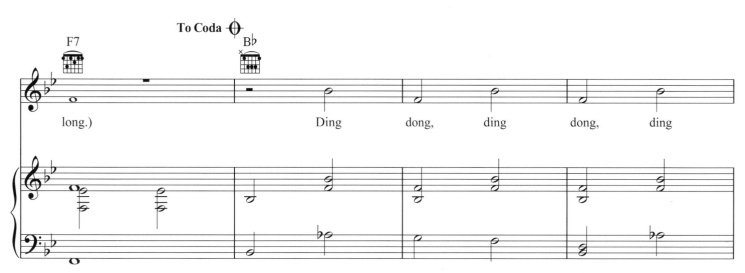

long.) Ding dong, ding dong, ding

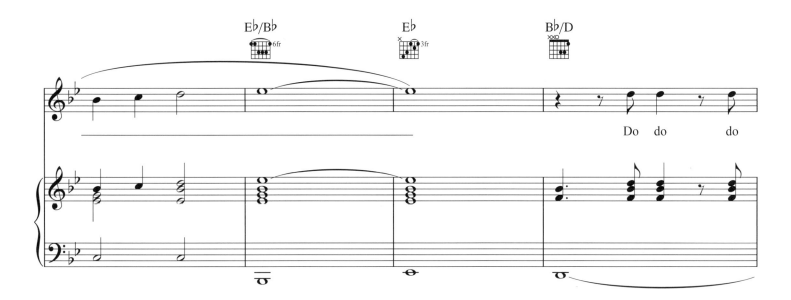

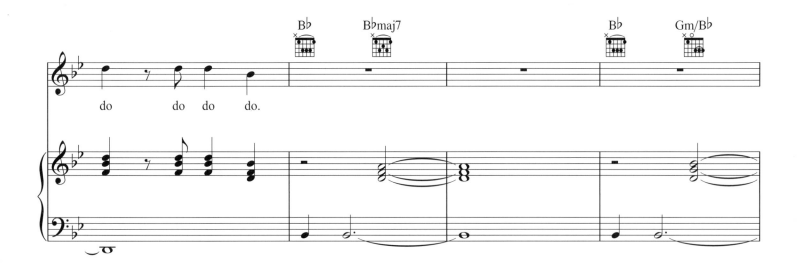

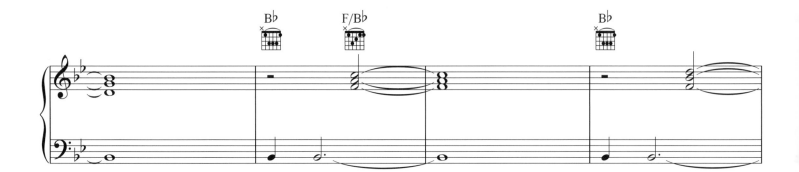

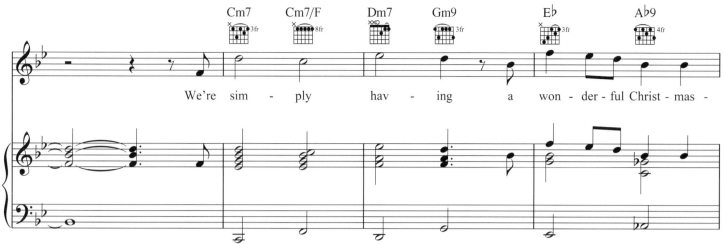

We're sim - ply hav - ing a won - der - ful Christ - mas -

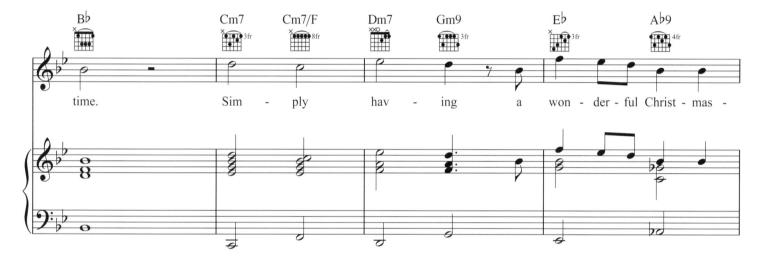

time. Sim - ply hav - ing a won - der - ful Christ - mas -

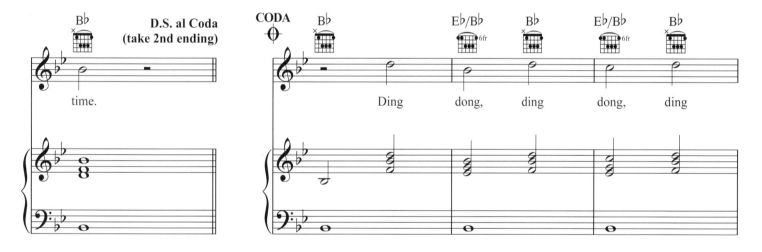

time.

D.S. al Coda
(take 2nd ending)

CODA

Ding dong, ding dong, ding

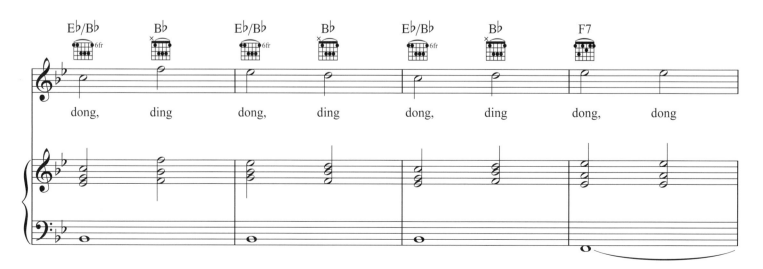

dong, ding dong, ding dong, ding dong, dong

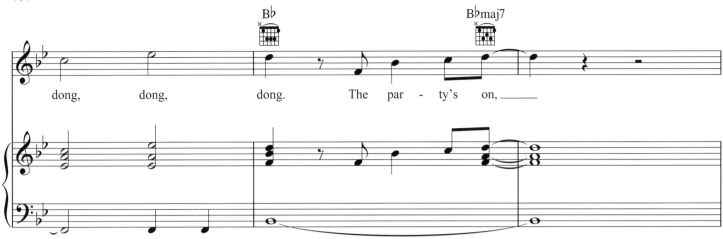

dong, dong, dong. The par - ty's on, _____

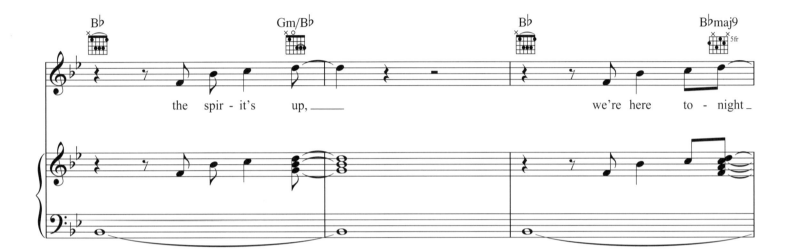

the spir - it's up, _____ we're here to - night _

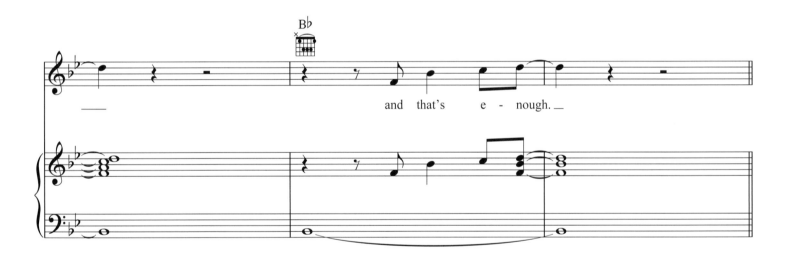

_____ and that's e - nough. _

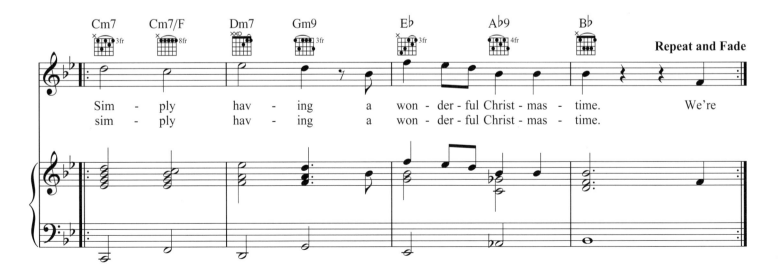

Sim - ply hav - ing a won - der - ful Christ - mas - time. We're

sim - ply hav - ing a won - der - ful Christ - mas - time.

Repeat and Fade